D0428582

DIPLOMACY in the DIGITAL AGE

diplomacy
in the
digital age

ESSAYS IN HONOUR OF AMBASSADOR ALLAN GOTLIEB

edited by
Janice Gross Stein
with **Colin Robertson**

SIGNAL
McCLELLAND
& STEWART

Signal is an imprint of McClelland & Stewart Ltd.
Signal and colophon are registered trademarks of McClelland & Stewart Ltd.

Library and Archives Canada Cataloguing in Publication

Diplomacy in the digital age / edited by Janice Gross Stein.

Includes bibliographical references.
ISBN 978-0-7710-8139-2

1. Diplomacy–Technological innovations. 2. Social media– Political aspects. 3. Technology and international relations.
I. Stein, Janice

JZ1405.D56 2011   327.20285'675   C2011-902106-4

We acknowledge the financial support of the Government of Canada through the Book Publishing Industry Development Program and that of the Government of Ontario through the Ontario Media Development Corporation's Ontario Book Initiative. We further acknowledge the support of the Canada Council for the Arts and the Ontario Arts Council for our publishing program.

Published simultaneously in the United States of America by McClelland & Stewart Ltd., P.O. Box 1030, Plattsburgh, New York 12901

Library of Congress Control Number: 2011931424

Typeset in Electra by M&S, Toronto
Printed and bound in Canada

ANCIENT FOREST
FRIENDLY

This book is printed on acid-free paper that is 100% recycled, ancient-forest friendly (100% post-consumer waste).

McClelland & Stewart Ltd.
75 Sherbourne Street
Toronto, Ontario
M5A 2P9
www.mcclelland.com

1   2   3   4   5   15   14   13   12   11

CONTENTS

DIPLOMACY IN THE DIGITAL AGE

Janice Gross Stein

Diplomacy functions best where it appraises and advises power, and does not attempt to substitute itself for the very real world of politics.

ROBERT BOTHWELL

Like authority, sin, Christmas, and winter, secrecy isn't what it used to be. Secrecy has lost its sanctity.

ANDREW COHEN

The diplomatic pouch has been torn asunder by the digital age, which is characterized by immediacy, transparency, profligacy, and universality. . . . In the digital age – building on the industrial age – we move from the some to the many, from the stately to the frenetic, from command to influence, from deception to candour, and from interests to issues.

WILLIAM THORSELL

Open diplomacy and open policy development – building vast global networks to harness ideas and nurture support everywhere, all the time – are the hallmarks of modern diplomacy.

ARIF LALANI

A remarkable group of scholars, essayists, and practitioners have come together in this volume to celebrate Allan Gotlieb's revolutionary contribution to the theory and practice of diplomacy in the last three decades of the twentieth century. They have come together to celebrate an outstanding intellect as well as a brilliant practitioner, a man who thinks lucidly and writes elegantly about diplomacy.

The contributors to this volume are also interested, as is Allan Gotlieb, in thinking forward about the future of diplomacy at yet another moment of significant change. Diplomacy is now being practised in the digital age. What does it mean to be a diplomat in a digitized world? What does a diplomat do differently in an age in which the information cycle spins continuously and hundreds of millions of people provide up-to-date information and engage in discussion through interactive social media? We asked our contributors to look back at Allan Gotlieb's seminal contribution in order to better understand the future.

This volume went to press in the aftermath of WikiLeaks and the beginning of the Arab Spring. WikiLeaks stunned the diplomatic community when it made public some of the more than a quarter million cables that it now has in its possession. Professionals worried actively about compromising sources, the threat to confidentiality, and the likely refusal of people to confide in diplomats now that there was no assurance that their identity would be protected. Secrecy, as Andrew Cohen puts it in his chapter, has lost its sanctity. How, diplomats worried, can they do their jobs, communicate confidential and valuable information, protect their sources, and provide the kind of analysis their governments need?

The public reaction to the leaked cables was quite different. Diplomats, people said with some surprise, are smart. "I didn't get much new information," one well-informed journalist told me, his voice tinged with envy and some uncertainty, "but, my God, diplomats write well." Seasoned observers were certainly titillated by the occasional surprising morsel of gossip and entertained by some of the fripperies. Overwhelmingly, however, they were engaged and impressed by the analyses that they read. Even within the skeptical and occasionally snooty academy, colleagues grudgingly acknowledged that "these diplomats" really do provide thoughtful and incisive analyses. Diplomats, in short, are not valuable because of the information they provide, but because of their authoritative knowledge and the quality of their analyses. Especially in a digital age awash in information, indeed drowning in information, knowledge and elegant analysis matter. They may matter even more than they did in the age of print, where editors traditionally assured the quality of what people read.

In the wake of WikiLeaks came the Arab Spring, one in a series of significant revolutionary waves in the digital age. Social media were important in helping demonstrators to organize, in feeding video to the world's media, and in giving a platform to the protestors as they struggled against governments who were desperately trying to close off global access to disturbing pictures and stories. Al Jazeera, the Arabic television station based in Qatar, provided saturation coverage of the protest movements, but often its journalists were denied access or expelled as contestation deepened. It too relied on social media for the critical content that it needed. Diplomats, at times removed from the pitched battles in the streets, were well behind the flow of information. They were not behind, however, in the analysis their governments needed as they struggled to craft responses to rapid developments in Tunisia, Egypt, Yemen, Bahrain, Libya, and Syria.

In a Paris hotel room late in the evening of March 17, 2011, the top U.S. diplomat struggled to coordinate the international response to the advance of Colonel Moammar Gadhafi's forces and the threat they posed to civilians in Benghazi, Libya. Initially opposed to any kind of military intervention, Secretary of State Hillary Rodham Clinton changed her mind after listening to some of her senior diplomatic advisers. She worked closely with the U.S. ambassador to the United Nations, Susan Rice, who had been urging a use of force to protect civilians from the vengeance of Gadhafi's loyalists. Rice worked the halls of the United Nations with classic diplomatic skills and promised the Secretary that she would get at least ten affirmative votes for a resolution that was far stronger than simply a no-fly zone. From Paris, Clinton worked to secure the support of Arab governments for the resolution that would be approved by the United Nations forty-eight hours later. It was this capacity to garner support for a strong resolution in New York at UN headquarters, as well as Arab engagement that persuaded President Obama to move ahead.

It was very much old-school, classical diplomacy – hands-on, informal, private conversations that put together the coalition in favour of intervention in Libya. Skilled diplomats worked the phones, called in favours, and kept their political leaders informed of which country was where on what issue. They built the coalition and drafted political leaders to make the important high-level calls that were necessary to cement the deal. In the midst of a revolution that got its oxygen from social media, the protestors in Benghazi depended on the skills of professional diplomats to survive.

These two vignettes bookend the themes of this book. When Allan Gotlieb was sent to Washington as Canada's ambassador three decades ago, he recognized immediately that the prevailing model of diplomacy would not be enough. Gotlieb continued to do what previous ambassadors had done, but also, as Marc Lortie tells us, vastly more. He reached out beyond the White House and the State Department to the Senate and the House of Representatives, to journalists and columnists and opinion makers, to the broad swath of people who influenced the open policy process with its many points of access in Washington. Sondra Gotlieb played a crucial part in this diplomatic transformation, becoming a Washington celebrity in her own right through her widely read column in the *Washington Post* and her talk-of-the-town parties.

How to manage the Canada-U.S. relationship remains a central question, perhaps even more complicated in the digital age than it was when the Gotliebs were in Washington. Colin Robertson looks at how the principles of Gotlieb's diplomacy travel forward into the future. Brian Bow, Jeremy Kinsman, and David Malone engage in a lively and vigorous debate about restructuring Canada's diplomacy as the world rebalances to include the newly rising powers of Asia and Latin America. How should Canada's diplomats continue to pay the United States the attention it deserves but stretch to make space for Asia, Africa, and Latin America? Does the digital age enable new kinds of Canadian initiatives in parts of the world where historically Canada has not been a significant presence? Can digital platforms compensate for scarce resources? Or is Canada simply too late to a worldwide party that is well under way?

Allan Gotlieb's practice of diplomacy was important not only for its remarkably innovative approach to the management of the Canada-U.S. relationship. It was also an early example of the "open diplomacy" in the contemporary period that Arif Lalani writes about. The broadening, widening, and deepening of diplomacy that Ambassador Gotlieb initiated in Washington is even more pressing today. In the digital age, William Thorsell argues, one-to-many – the printed word – and one-to-one – the telephone and telegraph – have been replaced by many-to-many communication. How do diplomats work in this age of distributed information?

In a related conversation, Kim Richard Nossal and Drew Fagan ask where headquarters is and what it looks like. Allan Gotlieb argued fiercely that the Department of Foreign Affairs should be a "central" agency, but in an era of distributed information, where is the centre? And what does the centre do? Elissa Golberg and Michael Kaduck write about the new kinds of interaction between headquarters and the field, and the ways in which Canada can leverage the many elements in its international toolkit. Finally, in a world where the centre is less central, Edward Greenspon asks who shapes the national interest, and what should it be? The essays in this volume deal with all these questions and more.

I do not want to prejudge the conclusions from the lively debates in which the contributors to this volume engage. Nevertheless, some broad themes that animate most essays pop up, even when the authors understand and develop their arguments quite differently from one another. These themes help to frame the debates that flow through this volume.

I would suggest that the core function of diplomacy remains as important as it has been traditionally. It is to provide experienced and thoughtful analysis, Denis Stairs argues, on policy options to leaders who have too little time to read, think, and consult before they have to make difficult decisions. Leaders can and do reach out beyond professional diplomats to seek opinions from a diverse group of people, but they have neither the time nor the attention to agglomerate these views, to sift, to dissect, to evaluate, and to bring to bear the relevant expertise. Diplomats are no longer principally conduits of information; in an information-rich age, this is no longer as necessary or as important. But diplomats, as the designers of web platforms say, "curate" the analysis and options for their leaders. Diplomacy functions best, argues Robert Bothwell, where it appraises and advises power. That is as true in the digital age as it was in the age of print and television.

But diplomats must do more. They must, as Allan Gotlieb did in Washington decades ago, reach beyond officials and traditional experts to tap into networks in the private and the nongovernmental sectors and draw upon the rich sources of information and policy analyses. Indeed corporations now conduct their own diplomacy, argues George Haynal, and function as autonomous actors in global politics. The debates that rage in the blogosphere are as lively and important as the opinions on the editorial pages of newspapers and, indeed, print and electronic media are becoming increasingly interwoven as they share content and inform discussion. As Arif Lalani suggests, diplomats can construct secure and open platforms to bring together experts and citizens from widely varying backgrounds to engage in deliberation. Here diplomats are enablers, but they are also agglomerators as they distill, organize, and analyze what they are hearing for their political leaders.

That diplomacy remains the same in the essential service it provides but is changing fundamentally in its practices suggests the creative tension, ambiguity, and even contradictions of the digital age. Diplomacy in the digital age will be both more open and more closed. It will be more open as it draws upon wider circles to inform thinking and analysis, but it will be more closed as it seeks to guard confidential analysis and secret information from leaks and disclosure. Less will be classified as secret, but more of what is classified will be stamped "top secret," unavailable to those who use freedom of information as a tool to lever information legitimately from government, as well as those who try to hack their way into government files.

Diplomacy in the digital age will be about influence with a far broader remit. Increasingly, embassies and consulates will become the integrated platforms to "brand" and market their country in a hypercompetitive environment. Diplomats will seek to influence not only foreign governments but also foreign business leaders, opinion makers, journalists, academics, and leaders of nongovernmental organizations. The best embassies will look more and more like Allan and Sondra Gotlieb's embassy in Washington.

Diplomats will face the challenge of organizing and integrating their work with other departments. Elissa Golberg, Michael Kaduck, and Drew Fagan write about the challenges of the "whole of government." As daunting as these trials are and continue to be, diplomats will likely face the even bigger challenge of the "whole of nation," drawing on the skills, expertise, and knowledge of individuals and groups outside government, and coordinating these to take the best possible advantage of the resources that citizens from a wide variety of backgrounds can bring to bear.

But diplomacy will also be about command. It was diplomats who put together the policy package for President Obama when he had to make the critical decision whether or not to commit U.S. military forces in Libya. States will always matter, especially when the use of force is an option, and where states matter, diplomats will be integrated into the command structure.

Diplomats and diplomacy are likely to be at the intersection of these competing trends that are working their way through the digital age. They are at the interface of openness and secrecy, of influence and command, of crowd sourcing and expertise, and of selling and representing. But most important, diplomats are at the intersection of screened information and intelligent analysis, where we need them most. As we have learned from Allan Gotlieb, even as our diplomats expand their responsibilities and broaden their networks, the best do thoughtful, perspicacious, and astute analysis extraordinarily well. Like Allan Gotlieb, they are irreplaceable.

part one
the art of diplomacy

ALLAN GOTLIEB:
A MIND IN ACTION

Robert Bothwell

Writing the biography of a living person is an exercise fraught with peril. With the dead, there is the time-honoured march of the obituary volume: solemn, respectful, worthy, and usually unsaleable. Such compositions slumber on top of the grave, like Cerberus on valium, simultaneously fierce and doze-inducing. It gets worse when the person to be biographied is not only alive but actively engaged in public life, adding elements of interest and controversy to a life that is very much not (as yet) fully lived. Inevitably, this is a limited biography, an introduction but not a conclusion.

That isn't to say that Allan Gotlieb has not already had a very full life. Born in Winnipeg in 1928, Gotlieb grew up in a family that derived from the Russian-Jewish emigration to North America. The Russian derivation was important for the isolated Jews of Winnipeg – 25,000 in a world they had to refashion for themselves, for many of the institutions of Winnipeg were barred to them. Unlike most Winnipeg Jews, the Gotlieb family was prosperous and could afford to live in the city's south end, rather than the immigrant north end – isolated outposts in a sea of Anglo-Saxon Protestants. As Gotlieb contemplated university – United College or the provincial foundation, the University of Manitoba – he saw more of the same. After two years at United College, therefore, he joined the exodus of talented Manitobans who abandoned the Blue Bombers and the Royal Winnipeg Ballet and the (eventual) Manitoba Theatre Centre for a kinder climate.

Much later, Gotlieb was asked why Winnipeg had produced so many talented people. "Why Athens?" he replied. One difference was that most Athenians stayed home. But Premier John Bracken, no matter how hard he tried, was not the new Pericles. Most Winnipeg ex-pats stopped in Toronto or Ottawa – journalist Larry Zolf, for example, or politician Jack Pickersgill in an earlier generation – but Gotlieb went one better, moving to the temperate zone in California, taking a gamble that there would not be an earthquake while he was there.

The University of California at Berkeley later earned a deserved reputation as a hotbed of radicalism in the seething sixties, but in the late 1940s it was still very much a product of the white-bread and white-skinned Anglo-Saxon West Coast, populated in its undergraduate aspect by young men and women who looked, dressed, and sounded as if they had just been released from a casting call for the Andy Hardy movies. But it was bigger and richer than the universities back home and, like other American schools, it had benefited from the migration of Jewish scholars from Hitler's Germany.

Gotlieb became a history student working under the émigré professor, Ernst Kantorowicz, who was teaching Byzantine history. Kantorowicz was a historian of the old school, with more than a touch of the Prussian in him. His depiction of the German past would, in another era, have harvested the good opinions of romantic German nationalists; as it was, he was fortunate to escape Hitler and the Nazis.

History, as encountered at Berkeley and later at Oxford, was in a particularly creative phase while Gotlieb was a student, stressing the mastery of complex and very detailed data in order to understand large phenomena. Sir Lewis Namier explained the politics of eighteenth-century England by reconstructing the interests and political factions of the reign of George III; as Gotlieb later put it, "to understand an era you have to disaggregate," to master microphenomena en route to understanding the larger picture. It was a technique he would revisit to understand American government and politics, and it still seems a serviceable tool for escaping the clouds of generalities that pass for academic analysis of politics.

In between Berkeley and Oxford, there was the Harvard Law School. Law, Gotlieb recollected, was "a secular choice," one he made in order to have a career. Law as taught and understood in the 1950s was close to history both in method and material: the development of the common law was taught from what were essentially history texts, while the case-study method required a mastery of detail and research that resembled the study of history. Harvard, like Berkeley, was close to its monochromatic past, an anteroom to the Supreme Court or to the great Wall Street firms for its brighter students. Gotlieb did very well, qualifying by Harvard's rules for the prestigious *Law Review* board, though not every course was successful – notably international law under Manley O. Hudson. Success at Harvard Law – despite Hudson – brought an offer from the New York firm of Sullivan and Cromwell, declined because Gotlieb had meanwhile captured a Rhodes scholarship to Oxford.

At Oxford, Gotlieb was awarded a fellowship at Wadham College, at the time notable for its historians, and passed the mid-1950s in England, pondering the law.[1] But the law was not by then his principal objective. Coming from a well-off family, he later commented, he was not particularly interested in money, and preferred the option of following "the best of [Canada's university] graduates going into public service," as the *Economist* put it.[2] And in the public service, it was the Department of External Affairs, Canada's foreign office, that had the highest reputation – the highest stature, as Gotlieb later put it. Indeed, "the best foreign service in the world," in the view of a friendly Oxford don.[3] In foreign policy, it seemed "the world was our oyster."[4]

Public service seemed a self-evident choice for a nation that had successfully organized its way through the Second World War, creating a small quiet pool of good government, in Isaiah Berlin's phrase. Mobilized for one war, Canada, like other western countries, stayed mobilized for the Cold War; its Foreign Service was part of that mobilization. The Foreign Service expanded rapidly, and Canada's visibility abroad spread too, especially at the United Nations, where the external affairs minister, Lester Pearson, was both prominent and effective. A Canadian presence was manifest in the opening (and sometimes closing) of embassies around the world, as Canada sought to reinforce on the ground a foreign policy that was of design and necessity multilateral. And so, in the 1950s, the public service was self-evidently successful. The Cold War supplied the underpinnings for an active foreign policy, while Keynesian economics, then at the height of intellectual fashion, supplied domestic policy.

Recruitment in Gotlieb's year did not involve an examination, but it did require appearing before a board of senior officers who would decide the suitability of candidates. Gotlieb's board was chaired by Norman Robertson, the former under-secretary, then serving as high commissioner in Great Britain. As Gotlieb recollected, the experience approached comic opera because Robertson lumbered into an interrogation regarding Gotlieb's grandparents, who had settled in Hirsch, Saskatchewan. Hirsch therefore qualified as ancestral turf, and Robertson probed Gotlieb's feelings about the place. He'd never been, the candidate replied, and no, he didn't have much interest in the place.[5]

Accepted nevertheless, Gotlieb arrived in Ottawa to take up his duties as a junior Foreign Service officer in 1957. Legal Division would eventually be his official dwelling, and King Edward Avenue, in easy walking distance of the office, the first of a series of Ottawa addresses he would share with his wife, Sondra, whom he had married in 1955. The department's Legal Division was his focus, and in and through Legal Division he met Marcel Cadieux.

Cadieux, assistant under-secretary in 1957, was the department's legal adviser and thus head of Legal Division; he had also served in a variety of posts in Europe, in Vietnam, and in Ottawa. A protégé of Norman Robertson, who was returning from London for a second tour as under-secretary, Cadieux was both influential and well positioned. He was, in Gotlieb's view, a "complete, ferocious peasant" in character, "shrewd and calculating."[6] Cadieux deeply admired Robertson, was devoted to the department, and to international law, which he taught on the side at the University of Ottawa. He also took an interest in Gotlieb, whose career he promoted.

International law was an obvious focus for the diplomacy of any well-prepared smaller power, like Canada. In a general sense, international law was, or could be, the key to stability and peace in international affairs. Canadian diplomacy promoted international law at a more practical and specific level. By establishing a framework of rules that applied to all nations, disparities in strength could to some extent be erased, or at least compensated for. For Canadian diplomats, what was meant by disparity was the relationship with the United States. And the model for coping was the diplomacy of the late 1950s that surrounded the revision of the Law of the Sea, where Canada carried, over American opposition, an expansion of territorial jurisdiction to twelve miles from three. Then and later, Gotlieb wrote, "We persistently sought international sanction, in the form of new rules, for actions that were strongly opposed by and largely directed against the United States."[7]

There was a limit to the use of international law, apparent to most international lawyers. As a practical matter, international law is an affair among consenting states.[8] Absent consent, relations revert to the standard and often rough practices of political diplomacy. In Gotlieb's view, some problems were better solved without recourse to arbitration or international tribunals or third-party mediation. That was especially the case in dealing with the United States. In fact, an arbitral tribunal theoretically did and does exist in Canadian-American relations – the International Joint Commission, established by the Boundary Waters Treaty of 1910. According to the treaty, the Canadian and American governments can refer any subject they choose to the commission; but in practice – very long-standing practice – references are kept infrequent and narrow, a fact that may explain why the commission is still in existence. Thus, although Canada won notable successes using international law as a tool, it could hardly be or become a principal goal of Canadian policy.

Canadians' focus on international affairs dwindled during the 1960s. In part, this was a reaction to a relative though not absolute diminution in Canada's standing in the international system, which meant that other countries could now afford to play a larger part in international affairs than they had been able to do in the years immediately after 1945. In part it was because Quebec was in danger of seceding from Canada, which necessarily concentrated scarce political and bureaucratic attention on the internal balance of the country.

The possible departure of Quebec placed French Canadians serving in the Ottawa government in a difficult position. Against the odds, they had found a place and a role in a predominantly English-speaking world. Marcel Cadieux, in particular, fiercely resented the notion that French Canadians should give up on Canada and seek their own destiny, not in Ottawa but in Quebec City. Cadieux was now under-secretary, succeeding Norman Robertson in the highest diplomatic office at Robertson's insistence. Gotlieb's career had moved in tandem with Cadieux's, and he was now legal adviser at a surprisingly young age, a fact that was naturally jealously noted in status-conscious and promotion-conscious Ottawa.[9]

The Quebec government was divided on how far to go in asserting the province's separate identity. Premier Jean Lesage was himself a fairly orthodox federalist, but several of his ministers and even more of his top-ranking civil servants envisioned an eventual separation and an independent Quebec. One means of achieving independence was by securing recognition as an independent actor in the international system, establishing autonomous links with foreign countries that could serve as precedents for repudiating Ottawa's jurisdiction in international matters. Foreign affairs was in this sense not an objective, but an instrument in the minds of Lesage's senior advisers. And yet securing concessions, one at a time, allowed the Quebec government to claim that Ottawa was jealously or irrationally blocking Quebec's practical, modest needs.

Gotlieb and Cadieux had no difficulty understanding Quebec's strategy. Pearson, now prime minister, and Paul Martin, minister of external affairs, came onside. In a white paper largely drafted by Cadieux and Gotlieb, the government asserted that only the federal government had an "international personality" and "exclusive responsibility for the conduct of external affairs as a matter of national policy affecting all Canadians."[10]

That was all very well in theory, but as a matter of practical politics, Quebec public opinion would not stand for Ottawa blocking contacts between the government of Quebec and the government of France on such sensitive matters as language and culture. Moving speedily, the Ottawa government placed Quebec-Paris relations in matters of culture under a kind of legal pre-clearance procedure. Ottawa gave advance approval to whatever Quebec and Paris might devise in the field in what was styled an "umbrella accord." Legal legerdemain had saved the day, or at least prevented a damaging precedent.

The confrontation over external powers underlined Ottawa's political weakness in the face of a potentially inflamed Quebec opinion. Recognizing that his government needed political reinforcement, Pearson reached out to prominent Quebec federalists to join his Liberal party and his Cabinet. Of these, the most unlikely was a free-wheeling Montreal intellectual, Pierre Elliott Trudeau, whose flinty personality and unorthodox habits alarmed more conformist politicians. They alarmed Cadieux too, who viewed Trudeau as a rich dilettante and playboy. But Cadieux and Trudeau were on the same side, and Trudeau proved to have both staying power and an icy magnetism that gave federalism a powerful and impressive spokesman in Quebec.

Appointed minister of justice by Pearson in 1967, Trudeau took over responsibility for constitutional negotiations among Ottawa and the provinces. Needing the strongest team possible, he drew on the available talent in all departments, and asked that Gotlieb be seconded to serve on it. (The two had met in 1965; at the time, Gotlieb probably thought Trudeau more decentralist than he was himself, in constitutional terms, but on the key question, Quebec, they were agreed.)[11] Serve he did, close enough to Trudeau to witness his successful candidacy for the Liberal leadership in the spring of 1968, and close enough to advise the new prime minister on the principles of the foreign policy he and Canada should adopt.

The installation of a new and strikingly different prime minister – Trudeau – might suggest that 1968 was a time of optimism, but in foreign affairs that was definitely not the case. The unpopular Vietnam War; despair over riots and disorder in the United States, in Europe, and even in Canada; the eruption of authoritarianism in many of the new countries of the Commonwealth; and paralysis in East-West relations all combined to sour the public mood. The 1967 Middle East crisis and the resultant Arab-Israeli war put paid to Canadians' pride over Pearson's signature accomplishment, the creation of a peacekeeping force to stand between Israel and Egypt in the Sinai. Canada's soldiers were ingloriously bundled out of Egypt amid a storm of abuse from the Egyptian government. Perhaps the fruits of peacekeeping, of mediation, of carefully cultivated impartiality were not so sweet after all.

Gotlieb sent his advice to Trudeau in the early spring of 1968. It would be an understatement to say it reflected the temper of the times.

To many Canadians, Canada has a moral obligation to help solve the problems of the world. Our culture, our character, our geographic location, our prosperity – all these and other factors have been thought to combine to endow us with a special role in helping to bring peace and sanity to the world.

What makes the decline of this role particularly serious for Canada is that it played an important part in forging our unity in the post-war era. Like the Danes who made good furniture, the French who made good wine, the Russians who made Sputnik, Canada, as a specially endowed middle power, as the reasonable man's country, as the broker or the skilled intermediary, made peace.[12]

It was an adept if ironic summary of the basic principles of Canadian foreign policy, as many and perhaps most Canadians understood them. The self-evident conclusion to Gotlieb's thought was that Canada could no longer afford to do all that, however noble the objective. Instead of "false internationalism," he recommended a more specifically self-interested approach to the world. He recommended more bilateral diplomacy, less emphasis on multilateral institutions, and less preachiness in support of unattainable goals. But he did not suggest that all Canada's goals and priorities were wrong – merely exaggerated.[13]

In some respects Gotlieb's arguments hearkened back to a concept, known as "functionalism," that the Canadian government had used to rationalize its quest for influence at the end of the Second World War. Broadly speaking, where Canada had an advantage and could make a contribution, it could in effect purchase a seat at the table. The doctrine could be, and was, used in an expansive way, but it can equally well be seen as a statement of limitations. Canada should concentrate its resources where it could make a difference and consequently have an influence. In terms of the late 1960s, those resources no longer sufficed to procure the influence Canadians expected but they could still be mobilized in more specific ways.

Gotlieb's advice pointed in a different direction than was imagined, nor did it paint a distant and pure isolationist mirage. He wanted to modify, not transform, to limit, not terminate. It helped his case that there were other forces and other priorities at work in Ottawa. Pearson in retirement was affronted by what he saw as too facile an identification of principled internationalism with rhetorical impracticality. The pursuit of difference, of change, might have been construed as self-interest, but it was not. The greater the change, in the opinion of most politicians and bureaucrats, the greater the risk. When the Cabinet considered a fundamental reorientation of Canadian foreign policy in March 1969, it did not think about it for long. Among other things, they had to contemplate, as Gotlieb later put it, "a geographical reality underlying Canadian foreign policy," and that was the United States.[14]

The great change in Canadian foreign policy that was anticipated under Trudeau thus never happened, as has been described elsewhere.[15] Trudeau did, however, shake up the foreign policy establishment, and, indirectly, Gotlieb's career. Cadieux had intended Gotlieb to be his successor as under-secretary, but when he encountered significant, indeed immovable, resistance, he suggested that his protégé instead become ambassador to the United Nations. When that too proved impossible, it was time for Gotlieb to go on his travels. He did become a deputy minister, but in the new Department of Communications – with Cadieux's sympathy and support. He would later move on to Manpower and Immigration, spending the nine years from 1968 to 1977 out of the diplomatic service.

External Affairs entered a troubled period. Trudeau's disdain for the department was clear enough, and manifest through his preference for advice and aid from a personal foreign policy adviser, Ivan Head.[16] Trudeau's choice as clerk of the Privy Council and head of the civil service, Michael Pitfield, used the department as a recruiting ground, moving its surplus (as he saw it) of talented people to other, less endowed agencies. Only when he saw that he might have gone too far, in 1977, did Pitfield consider reversing the process, and to do that he appealed to Gotlieb to return as under-secretary. Pitfield promised, in effect, to be good, and to do what he could to build up the department and enhance its role – to make it a "central agency," in the jargon of the day. There was a stronger minister of external affairs, Allan MacEachen, to whom Trudeau owed a notable debt of political gratitude. Together, a strong, if somewhat eccentric minister, and a strong deputy minister might pull off a reversal of fortune for Canadian diplomacy. And, nine years on, the resistance to Gotlieb from colleagues who thought he had once been promoted too far too fast had abated.

Gotlieb enjoyed a tumultuous four years as under-secretary. He served two governments, Trudeau's down to June 1979, Joe Clark's Progressive Conservatives from June 1979 to March 1980, and Trudeau's again for the balance of 1980 and 1981.

The Clark experience was none too happy, thanks to a clash with Clark's minister of external affairs, Flora MacDonald. As for the Trudeau years, Gotlieb had to deal with the Liberals' hyperactive return to power in 1980, when the government proposed to resolve Canada's financial problems, its energy difficulties, and its constitutional conundrums all at once. He had the unusual duty of asking the British government to withdraw its high commissioner to Canada, surely an all-time low in Anglo-Canadian relations. And he had to defend Trudeau's National Energy Program of 1980, which among other things interfered with existing property rights of American oil companies operating in Canada. Gotlieb and his department had to do it with one hand tied behind their collective backs, because they had been excluded from any role in drawing up the program, and hence had been unable to warn the government of its international impact.

In the face of rapidly deteriorating relations between the Trudeau government and the Ronald Reagan administration in Washington, the decision was made to send Gotlieb to Washington to explain and defend Canada's policies. Gotlieb has recorded the experience in a variety of places, especially in his *Washington Diaries* – a remarkable insight into the adaptive nature of diplomacy in averting confrontation if not catastrophe. Obviously, not only did Canada's diplomacy evolve, and with it Canadian policy, but also Gotlieb, whose job it was to master a new and complicated political and social environment, and to give Canada an identity, or a recognition, in a city and country where Canada is sometimes considered to be a folkloric fragment, or a reliable source of bad weather. In doing so, he and his wife Sondra expanded the nature of Canadian diplomacy in a city where the Canadian ambassador (with a couple of exceptions since the Canadian mission was opened in 1927) was usually a figure forgotten. Marcel Cadieux had discovered the problem to his sorrow when he arrived in Washington as Canadian ambassador in 1970. With much to say, he had almost no occasion to say it.

Gotlieb had also to master relations with the Progressive Conservative government of Brian Mulroney, who had driven the Liberals from office in the election of September 1984. As Gotlieb's diaries show, he fully expected to be fired, but he was not, remaining in his post and helping to pilot the Canadian-American Free Trade Agreement past the shoals of American – and Canadian – politics. He retired from professional diplomacy early in 1989, moving finally to Toronto where he and his wife added to the statistically significant number of Winnipeggers who had migrated to the bright lights of the Canadian metropolis.

Gotlieb spent his life not far from the centres of power, advising, proposing, disposing, and influencing. It was a life of active, not theoretical, diplomacy. At every point, when offering advice, Gotlieb pointed toward adaptation, to dealing with matters as they were. If that meant reducing or discarding past priorities, that was in the nature of the beast. Diplomacy functions best where it appraises and advises power, and does not attempt to substitute itself for the very real world of politics. It is not without its frustrations and very definitely not without its limitations. Diplomats like Gotlieb deserve respect, even affection, but also pity. As Malcolm Muggeridge once observed of a diplomatic friend who had come to see him off on a long train journey: "Poor Strang," Muggeridge wrote, "forever Jeeves to an increasingly demented Bertie Wooster."

Notes

1   See, for example, A.E. Gotlieb, M.A., "Intention, and Knowing the Nature and Quality of an Act," *The Modern Law Review*, 19 no. 3, (May 1956): 270–5.

2   1953 article, quoted in John Hilliker and Donald Barry, *Canada's Department of External Affairs*, vol. 2, *Coming of Age* (Kingston and Montreal: McGill Queen's University Press, 1995), 97.

3   The don was Stuart Hampshire, a noted philosopher. He praised in particular Paul Martin Sr.'s accomplishment, as head of the Canadian delegation at the UN, in breaking an impasse over the admission of new members such as Japan. On Hampshire's comment, see Allan Gotlieb, "The United States in Canadian Foreign Policy," O.D. Skelton Memorial Lecture, Toronto, December 10, 1991: available at http://www.international.gc.ca/odskelton/gotlieb.aspx?lang=eng. There were rivals to External Affairs, especially the Department of Finance, also at the height of its powers and reputation in the mid-1950s. Like External, it recruited among bright young university graduates, mindful of the high reputation certain Canadian economists enjoyed in the 1940s and 1950s. One, R.B. Bryce, clerk of the Privy Council in the late 1950s and later deputy minister of finance, was even credited with bringing Keynesianism across the Atlantic to Harvard.

4   Curiously, the view from inside the department of the new recruits was more skeptical – one head of personnel in 1952 minuted "it is by no means certain we are getting the best" (quoted in Hilliker and Barry, *Canada's Department*, 2, 59).

5   Gotlieb interview, March 10, 2011; Allan Gotlieb, *The Washington Diaries, 1981–1989* (Toronto: McClelland & Stewart, 2006), 15.

6   Gotlieb interview, March 10, 2011; Gotlieb added that, in terms of his interests, Cadieux was no peasant: he was a man with a very

sophisticated palate, with a deep knowledge of wines and gastronomy.

7   Gotlieb, Skelton Lecture. "No question," Gotlieb added in an interview on March 10, 2011, "I was committed to the view that it helps a nation state in dealing with a large power."

8   See Judith Shklar, *Legalism: An Essay on Law, Morals and Politics* (Cambridge, Mass.: Harvard University Press, 1964), 127–8; Gotlieb, Skelton Lecture.

9   See Christina McCall and Stephen Clarkson, *Trudeau and Our Times*, vol. 2 (Toronto: McClelland & Stewart, 1994), 210.

10 On the discussions between Ottawa and Quebec on this issue, see the exchanges in the *Globe and Mail* between Allan Gotlieb and Tom Kent, October 5 and 11, 2005.

11 John English, *Just Watch Me: The Life of Pierre Elliott Trudeau, 1968–2000* (Toronto: Knopf Canada, 2009), 132–33.

12 Gotlieb to Trudeau. The quote comes from a personal and confidential memo Allan Gotlieb sent Pierre Trudeau proposing a comprehensive review of Canadin foreign policy. At the time, Trudeau was minister of Justice and Gottlieb was assistant under-secretary of state for External Affairs. The memo was sent in the winter of 1967–68.

13 Gotlieb's memorandum "The Style of Canadian Diplomacy," has no date, but was written in early 1968; Gotlieb to author, April 29, 2003.

14 Gotlieb, "The United States in Canadian Foreign Policy," 7.

15 Robert Bothwell, *Alliance and Illusion: Canada and the World, 1945–1984* (Vancouver: University of British Columbia Press, 2007), chapter 15.

16 Head was known as Trudeau's "pocket Kissinger" among diplomats. Cadieux sarcastically called him "le professeur Head" referring no doubt to the cloudy and impractical views professors were known to carry – though Head had himself once been a professional diplomat, and only briefly a professor of law.

OBSERVATIONS OF A
SALOON KEEPER'S SPOUSE

Sondra Gotlieb

When my husband was serving as Canadian ambassador to
the United States, we entertained almost every day. And when
we weren't entertaining people at our residence, we were
going out to be entertained. It wasn't always that way. At first,
nobody wanted to come to the embassy and nobody asked us
out. The Canadian embassy had about a hundred and fifty
other foreign missions as rivals for Washington's attention, and
unfortunately, in terms of being an important destination,
according to Washington insiders, Canada's was considered
to be somewhere in the low-middle range. A knowledgeable
young congressional staffer once said to me, "Frankly, we
think the Australians are more interesting."

But according to the ambassadorial rulebook, we were supposed to entertain. Why else did we have a generous entertainment allowance? Why else did we have a butler and a
cook and an upstairs and downstairs maid and an extra little
fellow (I never really knew his job description) who swept
outdoors and acted as a waiter when we had guests? I soon
learned that they were not there for us; they were there for
the parties we were supposed to have.

Why was it so necessary to entertain? The sophisticated Sir
Nicholas Henderson, who was Britain's ambassador to the
United States when we arrived in the capital, explained the

reasons for embassy parties as something along these lines: "You have to reach out," he said, "because nobody knows where a political decision is being made in this town. If they tell you otherwise, they are either fools or liars." In other words, power is so diffused in the capital that looking for the decision maker is like searching through a thousand points of light (or darkness). Power is in the hands of the hundreds of congressmen and their staff, the lobbyists who write the bills for congressmen, the White House, the State Department, the Pentagon, the CIA, the Department of Agriculture, in fact, the whole alphabet of government agencies and institutions. There were always all kinds of political insiders (especially in the media) who knew (or claimed to know) someone who *really* knew what was going on.

The point of entertaining, I finally figured out, was to gather all these different power players together at *our* embassy so my husband could find out who was planning to do something that could possibly ruin something or someone in Canada – even if only through an unintended sideswipe. In the United States, Canada is very well liked and very easily forgotten. The latter, of course, is why we are so vulnerable to sideswipes – no one thinks of us when they are passing some nasty new law. We had breakfast meetings, literary lunches, and elaborate dinner parties so some politico would remember us when a decision was being made. Or so Allan could twist his arm. And of course, the ambassador should have some clue that somewhere in Washington's constellation of power a decision concerning his country was about to be made. The worst thing that could have happened to him – and his reputation – was if it became apparent that he was not in the know.

Dinner parties were usually the most important entertainments, but how do you get people to come when there is so much competition? In whose honour we would entertain was the most significant decision to make; that guest would be the magnet for other guests. The most unappealing guests of honour to American insiders were Canadian ministers of agriculture, health and welfare, transport – you name it – and, well, all other Canadian government officials, unless the individual had done something scandalous in public. A good Canadian guest of honour had to be famous: Pierre Trudeau or his wife Margaret, even though they were separated; Peter Jennings, a former Canadian who, at that time, was what I call an "Haute Media" star; Brian Mulroney; or, naturally, Wayne Gretzky. We managed to give dinner parties in honour of Trudeau, Jennings, and Mulroney, but Gretzky was too big for us. George Shultz, then secretary of state, was an admirer of the hockey star, and once watched Gretzky play from a special box arranged with our help, but I believe, *au fond*, our help was unnecessary.

George Shultz did seem to appreciate our attention, however, and became someone with whom Allan felt at ease. Actually, I don't think Wayne Gretzky had as much to do with their relationship as Ginger Rogers and Fred Astaire. An aide to Shultz casually mentioned to Allan one day that the secretary of state loved old Rogers and Astaire dance movies. So we'd set up a tacky screen in the living room and show films such as *Flying Down to Rio* and *Top Hat* to George and his wife Obie, as well as a handful of carefully selected guests.

The true significance of Washington social life and how it could be used as a tool to advance Canada's interests began to dawn on us after we observed the patterns of the powerful at parties. We soon noticed that the presence of the Haute Media at these events served as a magnet for high officials – and of course the press wanted to be with them in turn. Leaking to the press, we discovered, was one of the Reagan administration's standard methods of making and communicating government policy. It was a practice indulged in by several key administration players, each aiming to get his own position out or to discredit that of his rivals. Congressmen and their staffers had, of course, being doing this for years.

I recall coming home from a party at Pamela Harriman's, a socialite of international standing and, at the time, a prominent Democratic fundraiser. The party's obvious purpose was to raise money. I had been astonished to see a number of powerful Republicans in attendance. Joseph Kraft, the late *Washington Post* columnist, told Allan that, contrary to common belief in Washington at the time, the Reagan administration, including the Reagans themselves, was very interested in socializing and social climbing. In those years, unlike today, there were a number of prominent Georgetown hostesses, mainly Democrats, who entertained anyone who was in power, regardless of political stripe. This meant that they invited a lot of Republican senators and Cabinet secretaries. In turn, political players, lobbyists, and other influence-wielders, including powerful journalists such as Joe Kraft, David Brinkley, and Joseph Alsop, among many others, had a left-handed access to power. Allan was determined to have the same kind of access, on whichever hand.

A key reason for us to entertain was so that Allan could get a meeting with a senator or congressman who was trying to blockade our pork or potatoes for the sake of his state's pork or potatoes. Congressmen generally avoid meeting with ambassadors because it's a waste of their time since ambassadors can't vote or give money to their election campaigns. Parties got Allan around that obstacle.

Another reason to entertain was to promote tourism. Once there was a gas station owners' convention in Washington at the same time as a North American psychiatric gathering. For some reason, Allan was persuaded that we needed to entertain representatives of both groups. So we had the gas pump owners and the psychiatrists at the same time. I could see where the gas chaps benefited from tourism, but was hazy about the benefits the psychiatrists brought (and as a mere "wife of," it was not my role to ask). Nevertheless, the two groups got on very well. The psychiatrists tiptoed around, looking at Allan's collection of Tissot prints, and the gas station owners never bothered with the trays of drinks: they saved the waiters trouble by taking the bottles of liquor off the table and pouring their own. This is when I realized that, as the ambassador's wife, my role was to be the unpaid manager of a small saloon.

We knew, too, that we had to be careful about which Washingtonians we invited. The wife of a longtime American ambassador, and, at the time, important state department official, warned me when we arrived: "Watch out – don't get a reputation for entertaining embassy rats." I was shocked. "What or who are those?" I asked. She replied, "There are a lot of people in Washington with money who are not connected to politics. They have no interest in international affairs and no influence and don't know anyone useful to your husband. Canada means nothing to them. They just like going to embassy parties – any embassy. They want to be entertained. If you have too many of those people, you will get a reputation for giving parties for people who are not part of the political network. The embassy rats are of no interest to people like James Baker, Katharine Graham, Paul Volcker, Henry Kissinger – the decision makers your guests want to see." This was a very wicked remark and, unfortunately, true. So I rarely wasted Canadian taxpayers' money entertaining those in Washington society with no interest or connection to politics. Concentrating on VIPs did not always make us popular in certain circles in the capital, nor among vast numbers of visiting Canadians. (The only time we ever had Washington celebrities actually begging for an invitation was when the Cirque du Soleil came to town. Even Art Buchwald, who rarely went out, asked what he had to do to get a ticket.)

Upon their arrival in Washington, ambassadors' wives were invited to join ladies' luncheon clubs to meet Americans. The Cabinet wives were also invited to these luncheon clubs. Until then, I had never belonged to a ladies' luncheon club, and I thought the whole business was absurd. I doubt that they exist today, since there doesn't seem to be such a thing as an ambassador's wife any more (I coined the phrase "wife of" to describe the species), and if there is, she probably has a job. But I accepted the invitation to dine since I had nothing else to do. Allan urged me to go because he didn't even have a men's luncheon club to attend. It was there that I met Jean French Smith, the wife of the attorney general, who was a close friend of President Reagan. Jean French had as much disdain for the ladies' lunch as I did. But we attended despite our disdain, and we were both glad of it. She was from California and was as unfamiliar with Washington and its ways as I was. By that time Allan and I had realized that entertaining Canadian ministers and deputy ministers would attract only embassy rats. One day Allan said, "Let's have a dinner in honour of the Attorney General of the United States."

"But," I said, "you don't know him."

"I paid a courtesy call on him, and you know his wife; that's enough. But you have to ask her. I'm not going to ask him."

He bullied me into making that call; the first, but not the last, I ever made. She accepted, the invitations were sent out, and the guests included Ben Bradlee, Katharine Graham, and a third of Reagan's Cabinet, along with other Powerful Jobs and the Haute Media. Of course, I dropped a lot of names when I called and the list kept growing. That was another thing I discovered about entertaining: even if you have a social secretary at your disposal (the Canadian embassy employed one), if you are keen to have specific people attend your party, it's best to call them personally.

Allan believes he met most of his important contacts at Washington parties. VIPs told him some astonishing things about the White House attitude towards Canada while they were standing in our living room with a drink in hand.

That's why embassies entertain.

PUBLIC DIPLOMACY

Marc Lortie

Thirty years ago, Allan Gotlieb arrived in Washington to take up new responsibilities as Canadian ambassador to the United States of America. At the time, I was press secretary at the embassy and in that capacity I had the fascinating opportunity to observe how Allan, aided by Sondra, took public diplomacy to new heights. Washington was in transformation from the era of President Jimmy Carter to that of Ronald Reagan. Reaganomics, deregulation, and less government were the order of the day. The Canada-U.S. relationship was entering a zone of turbulence: Americans did not understand Canada's nationalist energy and economic policies. Canadian policies were seen as anti-American and Congress was ready to strike back. If relations were to become less fraught and more productive, Canada needed to implement a more modern form of diplomacy, one that was more public, more vocal. The embassy needed a new approach and Allan Gotlieb provided it.

Traditionally, embassies have worked mainly with governments. In Washington that meant working mostly with the administration, sometimes with Congress, and seldom with the media. But in the seventies, as a consequence of Watergate and the Vietnam War, Congress began asserting greater influence, notably in international affairs. At that time, the Canadian embassy had a small congressional relations unit, ably led by Georges Léger. But it was becoming clear that, to defend our interests, Canada needed to do more to engage both the Senate and the House of Representatives. We needed new alliances within the American political system and we needed to influence opinion makers.

During the Carter era, the Canada-U.S. relationship was generally harmonious. Trudeau's favourable disposition towards Jimmy Carter had been based on two factors. When France enunciated its new principle vis-à-vis Quebec of "*non-ingérence, non-indifférence,*" Carter spoke out in favour of Canadian unity; a very important political gesture given that the Lévesque government was planning a referendum on the future of Quebec during its first mandate.

Second, Carter was prepared to move quickly to deal with a long-standing irritant: the share of fisheries of the East Coast and the delimitation of the Gulf of Maine maritime boundary.

The Canadian government had appointed Marcel Cadieux the chief negotiator opposite the U.S. government's Lloyd Cutler, a well-known Washington power broker. Allan Gotlieb admired Marcel Cadieux greatly. Both were trained in law and Cadieux had recruited Gotlieb into External Affairs. Gotlieb admired Cadieux's incisive mind and mastery of foreign policy. Cadieux was hard working, forward looking, innovative, decisive, tough minded, and a great raconteur, all things one can also say about Gotlieb.

After two years of difficult and intense negotiations, a treaty was finally completed and signed by both leaders, and then sent to Parliament and the U.S. Senate for ratification. The Canadian Parliament proceeded quickly, thanks mainly to the fact that all stakeholders, including East Coast parliamentarians, fishermen, and provincial governments, had been kept informed and were fully involved in the negotiation process. On the U.S. side, it was a different story. After a long delay, the administration finally sent the treaty to the Senate, which failed to pass the treaty. Local interests trumped the national interest, as is often the case in Congress. Canadians were stunned and the government was flabbergasted. How could it be that a Democratic Congress could fail to pass a treaty negotiated and proposed by a Democratic administration and a Democratic president?

Welcome to Washington politics. Canada needed to review its way of doing things in Washington. Times had changed. Was Allan Gotlieb, senior mandarin, Oxford graduate, cultivated art collector, and man of influence close to Trudeau, properly suited for the job? The Canadian media were skeptical. They, and we at the embassy, would quickly find out.

Ronald Reagan arrived in Washington in January of 1981 with an agenda to restore the American economy and America's place in international affairs. At the time, Americans were pessimistic about their economic future; Japan was perceived as the economic engine of the world, taking Hollywood, New York, and Detroit by storm. Americans were also concerned about their place in the world; the Iranian hostage crisis had taken a toll on America's psyche. The old American reflex of isolationism was re-emerging. In the United Kingdom, Margaret Thatcher, elected two years previously, was imposing her tough economic policies on Britain and battling the powerful British trade unions. Helmut Schmidt was presiding over an increasingly self-confident West Germany. France had elected François Mitterrand, its first Socialist president since the 1936 *Front populaire*. In Canada, in response to the 1980 Quebec referendum that shook Canadian unity, Prime Minister Pierre Trudeau was engaged in a nation-building exercise, concentrating on the patriation of the constitution, a new charter of rights, and the establishment of nationalist energy and investment policies, known as the National Energy Program (NEP). Trudeau and his energy minister, Marc Lalonde, thought that the NEP would have the same therapeutic effect as the 1962 creation of Hydro-Québec which had allowed Quebeckers to feel *"maîtres chez nous."*

In 1981 Canada also hosted, for the first time, the G-7 Economic Summit, which took place in June at Montebello. Gotlieb, then under-secretary of state for external affairs, was appointed by Trudeau as the summit "sherpa" – that is, the senior official responsible for policy and other preparations for a meeting of heads of government. The Montebello summit was deemed a success, not only in terms of progress on North-South issues and East-West discussions, but also in terms of Canada's capable organization of a major international meeting. However, the Montebello summit would be remembered by many for having been the *entrée en scène* on the world stage of Ronald Reagan. At the summit, "Reaganomics" was sold by the new president's effective "spin doctors": Ed Meese, Richard Allen, and Larry Speakes. The Quebec press paid particular attention to the meeting between François Mitterrand and René Lévesque to see whether the new U.S. president would side with the Quebec nationalists.

It was a major relief to some and a great disappointment to others to discover that the French president had no disposition to support the independence of Quebec.

In his role as sherpa, Allan Gotlieb observed first-hand the Reagan White House in action: a scripted president, aided by an aggressive messaging operation, selling the American perspective to world audiences. What happens *inside* a meeting room is often not as important as what emerges *from* the meeting – which version of the outcome is accepted and disseminated. It made an impact on Gotlieb.

Prior to his Washington assignment, Allan Gotlieb had been one of Ottawa's most senior mandarins, highly respected by both the political level and the bureaucracy, but not a public persona. In Ottawa, the role of the senior civil servant was, and still is, to provide the best possible advice to his or her political masters, not to engage with the media. In Washington, Gotlieb would have to change gears: go public, assume a new high-profile public role, make speeches, speak on record to the media, give interviews, all to sell the Canadian perspective.

By the time Gotlieb arrived in Washington in October of 1981, the bilateral relationship was tense on multiple fronts: acid rain, trade irritants, protectionist bills, energy and investment policies, and a more ideological White House. In addition, Quebec was perceived, in the words of William Safire of the *New York Times*, as the "Cuba of the North."

It was difficult, indeed almost impossible, to get the Canadian message onto the crowded American political radar screen, and when Canada did get mentioned, our policies were characterized as anti-American, nationalistic, sometimes even socialist – a bad word in the American lexicon, then as now. Gone was the euphoria we had known in 1979 when Canadians were celebrated as heroes after the "Canadian caper," when Ken Taylor and his team had engineered the escape of American hostages from Tehran. It became evident that success in the new Washington environment would be defined by how successful you were in making your policies publicly known; how successful you were in reaching out to influential opinion leaders, senior journalists, and columnists; how successful you were in influencing the fourth pillar of the American political system: the media.

There was plenty of talent at the embassy ready to assist Gotlieb in pushing back against the anti-Canadian voices: Gerry Shannon, the experienced "number two" in charge of the economic and trade issues; Jeremy Kinsman, head of the political section and one of our best foreign policy minds; George Rejhon, who was more knowledgeable about acid rain than most environmental NGOs; Patrick Gossage, head of Public Affairs, freshly recruited from Trudeau's office where he had been press secretary; Gary Soroka, a masterful speech writer; and me, the press officer.

Our role as the embassy team was to develop a strategy to raise Canada's profile on issues of importance to our national interest and to ensure that the new ambassador delivered that message not only to the media and administration and the Congress in Washington, but across the whole country. We quickly learned that the Gotliebs were up to the challenge.

Not long after the Gotliebs' arrival, the *Washington Post* expressed interest in having an editorial board meeting with the new ambassador. My interlocutors at the *Post* were John

Anderson on the editorial page and Dusko Doder, a veteran reporter on the international desk who set this meeting up. Katharine Graham, the publisher and one of the most influential women in Washington, rarely attended the board meetings, but this time she made an exception and decided to host the Canadian ambassador for a luncheon in her private boardroom. Needless to say, everybody on the editorial board and the international desk accepted the invitation. Katharine Graham was not as intimidating as Ben Bradlee, her celebrated executive editor. She was rather a matter-of-fact person, with a deep interest in understanding issues – on this occasion Canadian cultural policies concerning foreign magazines. Allan described the rationale for the Canadian policy brilliantly, explaining why Canada found it necessary to defend Canadian cultural products. Allan was, as usual, well prepared and articulate, ready to defend Canadian policies and to push back on any aggressive line of questioning. Graham was impressed by his line of argumentation. She was also impressed by Allan's explanations of other Canadian policies concerning trade, the environment (e.g., acid rain), or foreign relations, all perceived as anti-American. Bradlee was also very positive after this first encounter. Allan had established himself as a knowledgeable and credible interlocutor. Word got around Washington pretty quickly. The Canadian ambassador was really worth talking to!

Shortly thereafter, the style section, a widely read section of the *Post*, came out with a front-page story on Sondra, the writer and the "wife of" the new Canadian ambassador. Sondra had an important impact in our public diplomacy efforts. With her wit and her non-diplomatic *franc-parler* she soon became the darling of the Washington media. Her friendships with Polly Kraft, wife of Joe Kraft, one of the most influential political columnists in Washington, and with Meg Greenfield, editor of the editorial page of the *Post*, gave her marvellous access. It was Greenfield who proposed that Sondra write a regular humorous column on the newspaper's op-ed page entitled "Wife Of." Sondra became an overnight media star, catapulting Canada into a unique sphere of influ-- ence in Washington, which benefited all of us at the embassy.

The embassy developed a strategy to reach out to reporters, columnists, TV anchors, the border papers, and the Canadian press reporters. For two years, I witnessed first hand how Allan Gotlieb reached out to important opinion leaders throughout the U.S., giving "on the record" interviews, making time to sit down with reporters for background briefings, hosting numerous working breakfasts and luncheons with groups of reporters, always with the objective of explaining and putting Canadian policies in perspective. It was part of his daily agenda. At every major event they hosted, the Gotliebs ensured that journalists were on the guest list. Gotlieb was a uniquely well-informed interlocutor on foreign policy issues to Washington's most influential journalists: Joe Kraft, James (Scotty) Reston, Jim Hoagland, David Broder, William Safire, Ben Bradlee, Robin McNeil, Jim Lehrer, Hedrick Smith, Hobart Rowen, and Don Oberdorfer, all powerful voices that helped shape the U.S. political agenda. The Gotliebs embodied public diplomacy at its finest hour.

In Reagan's Washington, if you were talked about in the media, people wanted to meet you, so Gotlieb received constant invitations to speak, and it was up to us to pick and choose the best forum for delivering our message. A classic Gotlieb speech always contained four elements: the importance of a level playing field, especially in trade and economic matters; the importance of establishing a rules-based relationship between partners; the concept that "cultural sovereignty or identity" was as fundamental to Canadians as the concept of "national security" was to Americans; and finally, that Americans could not find better allies and closer friends than Canadians. Those four themes constituted the core Canadian message to American audiences. Once Gotlieb approved a final version (usually only hours before the event), my role as press officer was to sell the speech to reporters. We needed friends in the American media and David Shribman, at the time a young reporter in the Washington bureau of the *New York Times*, was one of these friends. His insightful coverage of the ambassador's speeches, particularly at the beginning of Gotlieb's mandate, made an enormous impact on Allan's reputation in Washington political circles.

Sometimes we got carried away in our enthusiasm. I remember the first visit we organized for our new ambassador to the West Coast. With the former governor of California in the White House it was important that the new ambassador establish his bona fides there, and so Los Angeles, San Francisco, and San Diego were essential destinations. Each visit included six elements: a speech at a major forum such as the Chamber of Commerce or the Commonwealth Club; calls on influential political figures (it was often more effective to meet a senator or congressman on his home territory than in Washington); an editorial board meeting with the local paper (we knew that these were read closely in the White House); an interview with local television or a morning radio talk show; and a visit to a university campus to meet students in Canadian studies.

In San Francisco, in order to emphasize the Canadian connection, Kinsman, Soroka, and I, as baseball fans, engineered a visit to coincide with the opening of the 1982 baseball season. The Giants were hosting the Montreal Expos. I do not recall how we convinced the management of the San Francisco Giants to greenlight it, but the Canadian ambassador was invited to throw the first ball. What we didn't know was how bitterly cold Candlestick Park could be in the month of April. The other thing we didn't know was how inexperienced Allan was as a baseball pitcher! His valiant effort at a pitch failed to reach home plate and our ambassador was booed by the San Francisco fans. So much for our brilliant idea. We learned our lesson: avoid exposing Allan Gotlieb to sporting activities, and maintain the focus on all those areas where his wit, wisdom, and knowledge served Canada so well.

The year 2011 marks the centenary of Ronald Reagan's birth and Americans are celebrating his achievements. Allan and Sondra Gotlieb were among the closest observers of the Reagan White House and as such, were able to make a great contribution to the promotion of Canada's interests. The art of diplomacy involves penetrating a foreign environment, understanding a government's priorities and preoccupations, and picking up signals on a broad range of subjects. It involves building bridges between governments and nations on the basis of that knowledge and understanding.

Apart from Allan Gotlieb, few on the Canadian side picked up the important signal that Ronald Reagan sent to Canada in launching his presidential campaign in 1979. He spoke of a North American accord and improved relations with both neighbours, Mexico and Canada.

It took Brian Mulroney, a sure-footed and confident Quebecker, to change the trend in the Canada-U.S. relationship. In 1984, the new prime minister was inspired when he decided to keep Allan Gotlieb in Washington. Mulroney did not have a grand design for a free-trade agreement with the U.S. but he knew that the NEP was not a policy that would convince Quebeckers to remain attached to Canada. Mulroney understood the desire of a young generation of Canadians, including Quebeckers, for greater prosperity. He moved fast to build a more confident bilateral relationship. In order to do so, he listened carefully to the signals his ambassador picked up in Washington. Soon, Gotlieb would become a key player in the negotiation, ratification, and implementation of a Canada-U.S. free trade agreement that led to NAFTA and greater prosperity for Canadians.

In a city like Washington, it does not take long to know whether you can cut it or not. In the dining room of the official residence, the walls lined with their collection of Tissots, the Gotliebs entertained *la crème de la crème* of official Washington. A steady stream of Canadian leaders, provincial premiers and ministers, and others were thus given an opportunity to meet and influence key American decision-makers and opinion formers. Thus public diplomacy was born and brilliantly implemented by Allan Gotlieb.

part two
Canada's diplomatic
challenges: continuity and change

CHANGING CONDITIONS AND ACTORS, BUT THE GAME REMAINS THE SAME:
Revisiting Gotlieb's "New Diplomacy"

Colin Robertson

It began with bitter disappointment. In good faith and in classic diplomatic fashion the Canadian legal team, led by the iron-willed Marcel Cadieux, who had served as ambassador to Washington from 1970 to 1975, had negotiated at length with the Carter administration, and finally signed, in March, 1979, an East Coast Fisheries Agreement and a companion Maritime Boundaries Treaty.

We knew that the U.S. Constitution required that all treaties be subjected to Senate ratification but, as Cadieux would later tell a group of us junior officers, the assurance from the administration was that it would happen. It didn't. A member of the U.S. Senate Foreign Relations committee, the courtly and aristocratic Senator Clairborne Pell, put a hold on its consideration because of the unhappiness of a few hundred scallop fishermen from his home state of Rhode Island. Teddy Kennedy, who was challenging Jimmy Carter for the Democratic presidential nomination at the time, supported Pell. The administration chose not to press and the Canadian treaties were subsequently withdrawn from consideration.

It was a stark lesson in American politicking and the influence of local interest, and a vivid example of the separation of powers between the Executive Branch and Congress.

———

For Allan Gotlieb, the new under-secretary of state for external affairs, it was also a wake-up call. Mandated by Prime Minister Trudeau to make the Foreign Service more relevant, Gotlieb decided that we would have to significantly change our approach to the conduct of diplomacy in the United States. In foreign policy terms, Gotlieb would observe, "there is the United States . . . then there is the rest."

When Arnold Heeney, twice Canada's ambassador to the United States (1953–57, 1959–62), had a problem with Congress, he'd gone to see his friend Willis Armstrong, who manned the Canada desk in the State Department. As Gotlieb would later relate in conversation in February, 2005:

*"And he [Heeney] said, "Oh, Will, we've got a problem.
Some of your senators are trying to suck the water out of
the Great Lakes. They will affect the water levels, what do
I do?"
"Well, I think you have to go on the Hill and talk to them."
"Who do I see?"
And he said, "I think you should see Lyndon Johnson, the
Senate majority leader."
Arnold asked, "Do you think you can get me an appointment to
see him?"
Will said, "Sure, I can manage that." So he called Lyndon
Johnson, and he received Arnold Heeney.
Johnson said, "What can I do for you, boy?"
Heeney said, "Well, we have a problem."
"What's your problem, boy?"
"Well, some of your congressmen – senators – have this bill
proposed that would be very bad for Canada: it's going to
affect the water levels. That's the problem."*

Lyndon Johnson said, "No. You don't have a problem."
Arnold said, "I just explained to you. I have a problem."
"No. I just solved it. That bill's dead."

Those days were gone.

Gotlieb's "new diplomacy" would upset what he described as the commandments of traditional diplomacy: "Thou shalt conduct all official business through the intermediary of the foreign ministry . . . Thou shalt not intervene in the domestic affairs of the country to which thou art accredited."

The doctrine of separation of powers and the fragmentation, diffusion, and atomization of those powers within Congress means, in practical terms, that a foreign ambassador to Washington is accredited less to a government than to a system. As such, he and his team join a constellation of players: the members of Congress and their staff, the administration and its agencies, the lobbyists, lawyers, think tanks, media, and other special interests that are "constantly shifting, aligning, and realigning" around Capitol Hill. Within this system, a foreign power is just another special interest, and lacking the tools of money or votes, not an especially special one.

One of Gotlieb's first innovations was to make congressional relations part of the job responsibilities for junior officers heading out to their first assignments in our U.S.-based consulates. We were to get to know their local staff and advocate for Canadian interests. As one of that first wave of Gotlieb "acolytes," I met with a young Chris Dodd, newly elected member of Congress from Connecticut (later chair of the Senate Banking Committee), with Charlie Rangel (later chair of the House Ways and Means Committee) in his Harlem office, and with Tim Russert, then a principal aide to Senator Daniel Patrick Moynihan of New York (later host of NBC's *Meet the Press*). This was "long-game" diplomacy and the connections would serve me well years later when I was posted to Washington as head of the new Advocacy Secretariat (2004).

When he was appointed to Washington, Gotlieb, who would become our longest serving envoy (1981–89), applied his "new diplomacy" with vigour and success. In diplomatic terms, the change in approach was tectonic. Capitol Hill had been considered off limits, but now we were playing the game the way the Americans played it, and since we couldn't offer either campaign contributions or votes, it required skill and finesse.

In a series of lectures, later collected in *I'll Be with You in a Minute, Mr. Ambassador: The Education of a Canadian Diplomat in Washington,* Gotlieb spelled out his "decalogue" for the conduct of the new diplomacy:

1. The particular process by which a decision is reached in Washington is often so complex and mysterious that it defies comprehension.
2. The most important requirement for effective diplomacy in Washington is the ability to gain access to the participants in the decision-making process.
3. Given the vast numbers of players in the field of decision making, and the great difficulty of predicting their likely behaviour, the highest possible premium must be placed on political intelligence.

4. Since there are so many participants in decision making, so many special interest and pressure groups, and so many shifting alliances, a diplomat cannot design any grand or overarching strategy to further his nation's interests. Every issue involves its own micro-strategy and every micro-strategy is unique.

5. In Washington, a foreign power is itself just another special interest, and not a very special one at that.

6. A foreign power, as a general rule, has no permanent friends or adversaries on Capitol Hill.

7. A foreign power, as a general rule, has no permanent friends or adversaries within the administration.

8. No permanent solutions are within reach of the ambassador or his government, only temporary ones. Instability is the norm, alliances and coalitions are always being forged, forces and counterforces are always mounting.

9. Effective diplomacy means public diplomacy. The line between public diplomacy and interference in local affairs is a thin one and thus diplomacy must be practised with considerable finesse.

10. The best and often the only way to gain access to key players is through the social route. In Washington, parties are a continuation of work by other means.

I would keep copies of *I'll Be with You in a Minute: Mr. Ambassador* on my desk at both the office and at home. It was the single best guide to doing business in Washington. My Mexican counterpart, a former legislator, also looked to it as "the source." I later learned that the Japanese had translated it as a guide for their Washington-bound diplomats. Even today, the New Zealand ambassador to the U.S., former prime minister Michael Moore, keeps a copy at hand and he's told his young staffers "not to read it at night as they won't be able to sleep."

Gotlieb's new diplomacy delivered

There were notable results in terms of sovereignty – acknowledgement of our jurisdiction in the Arctic – and the environment – negotiation of the Acid Rain Accord and Great Lakes cleanup. The game changer, however, was the negotiation of the Canada-U.S. Free Trade Agreement in 1988, and it would not have happened if we had not mastered the art of congressional diplomacy. Passage in the Congress was no sure thing in either the finance committee or the full Senate. It ushered in an era of prosperity and gave Canadians confidence that they could compete internationally. We have since become not just a trading nation, but a nation of traders.

The "jointness" of the increasingly integrated North American supply chains means that today, intra-firm trade, from General Motors to General Electric, accounts for a third of Canada-U.S. commerce. Nearly 70 per cent of bilateral trade is intra-industry: transportation, manufacturing, and energy. More remarkable, domestic content in Canadian manufactured goods has dropped below 50 per cent as the process becomes that of making things together rather than just trading things.

Integration is most apparent between states and provinces and, increasingly, at the municipal level as American and Canadian jurisdictions deal together with issues of trade, transportation, energy, and the environment. This has created a network of official relationships at the substate level – through, for example, meetings of governors and premiers and regular conferences of legislators that constitute the "hidden wiring" of the relationship. These official interactions are supported by non-official relationships that include professional and amateur sports, business, and education, as well as the estimated million "star-spangled" Canadians who live and work in the U.S.

In the years since Gotlieb left Washington, one event and a series of related developments have further complicated the conduct of diplomacy. September 11, 2001 (commonly referred to as 9/11) changed America. We live in an age of terror. Americans see themselves as the primary target in what is likely to be a long and shadowy war. The existential threat is fundamentally changing American society and government. Security *does* trump all, and before Americans will be prepared to lift the drawbridge at what has become a real border, they will have to be satisfied that Canadians take security as seriously as they do.

Second, the Internet and the rise of YouTube, blogs, and tweets have further democratized and atomized the political process. In Gotlieb's era, he knew the dozen lobbyists in Washington that counted. There are now over 33,000 in the capitol. This explosion in the number of lobbyists and means of communication underlines the need for public diplomacy and the requirement for "rapid response" within the same media cycle – and media cycles are growing ever faster.

Third, the American political process has become polarized and even more partisan. The seismic shift wrought in 1994 with the election of Newt Gingrich and the GOP's "Contract with America" has only deepened the cleavage between the parties and the political weight of the most passionate. "It's not just a tug of war between left and right," writes *New York Times* columnist Charles Blow (April 3, 2010). "It's a struggle between the mind and the heart, between evidence and emotions, between reason and anger, between what we know and what we believe." American politics, observes the *National Journal's* Ron Brownstein (February 24, 2011), "increasingly resembles a kind of total war in which each party mobilizes every conceivable asset at its disposal against the other. Most governors were once conscientious objectors in that struggle. No more." As the non-partisan Pew Foundation's comprehensive survey of voters (May 4, 2011) concludes, most politically engaged Americans are opposed to compromise, divided on most national issues, and increasingly separated by everything from their race to their choice of news source.

Fourth, the FOX effect. Reflecting the breakdown in elite consensus, which arguably made it easier to do business in Washington, as well as the political polarization, there is the phenomenon of the FOX Network. Taking its inspiration from the lively, opinionated penny papers of an earlier empire, it has found its niche – "half of America," as Charles Krauthammer told me. Canada needs to exercise special care because we can become a surrogate for two of FOX's perennial peeves: first, the "cheese-eating, socialist, surrender monkey" Europeans and, second, the "porous border," because criticism of Canada is seen to balance the ongoing criticism of Mexico over the smuggling of drugs and people and the reportage of corruption within Mexico.

The continuing dispersal of power, the legions of special interests armed with cheque books, and the increasing left-right polarization accentuate the challenges of doing business in the United States. But Canadians can still make headway in this evolving system by keeping in mind this coda to the Gotlieb Decalogue.

1. Understand the American system, especially Congress.

Too often we transpose our Canadian mindset to the American system. It's not the same.

The founding fathers of America created a system of brokerage politics with a separation of powers and checks and balances designed to frustrate radical change. It makes for an irrational policy-making environment that can be confusing for those used to the Canadian variation on Westminster-style government.

The founders put strict constitutional curbs to prevent king-like tendencies in their presidency. However, the presidency continues to be our best entrée into the U.S. system because the office, unlike the Senate or House of Representatives, is purposely designed to put the national interest above regional and local interests. The power of the presidency lies less in its constitutional authority than in its "bully pulpit" ability to appeal to the national interest, an ability that is progressively enhanced by the medium of communications from the "fireside" radio chats of Franklin Roosevelt through John F. Kennedy's televised address to the nation to the contemporary usage of YouTube by Barack Obama.

Congress, by the founders' design, is the first branch of American government. In relative terms, members of Congress have much more power and influence than members of Parliament. Congressional dominance is the normal condition for American democracy, except during periods of war or international tension, when an external challenge induces congressional deference to the executive. Committee and subcommittee chairs are like medieval barons: they propose and dispose, and they can literally write the law of the land.

In his elegant memoir, *America at Century's End*, former Secretary of Defense James Schlesinger recounts this advice from Bryce Harlow, the canny advisor to Presidents Eisenhower and Nixon, to those new to Washington: "Whatever you may think of the intelligence of those in Congress, the Congress has immense power. If you provoke it sufficiently, it can rear back and strike you. It can destroy an administration. Never underestimate the Congress."

2. Know your "ask." Frame it as an American issue and play by their rules.

America's most popular sport is football. It may lack the elegance of hockey or baseball, but a lot of the football playbook has application when working on Capitol Hill. Much of the congressional legislative process is similar to "three yards and a cloud of dust." The system is designed for "block and tackle." An average of eleven thousand bills are introduced each Congress. Less than five hundred of them reach the president's desk for signature or veto.

On almost any issue, and especially in the case of the environment, we have more friends and allies than we realize or appreciate. Too often, when seeking relief from an American action, we have not thought through what we really want or can offer up in return. After a particularly difficult session with a visiting delegation, a congressman turned to me in frustration and said, "You look like us, you sound like us, but you can be more opaque than the Chinese."

Americans usually know exactly what they want, and they have little patience to either interpret or wait while we figure out our "ask." Canadians also have a tendency to negotiate first with ourselves and, in the process, to ask for what we think we will get rather than what we really want.

Asymmetry in population usually means that more Americans think like Canadians than there are Canadians. On almost any issue you can find an American ally with whom you can make common cause. We must always avoid making it personal, because an adversary on one issue can be an ally on another.

This asymmetry means we play by their rules. As Ambassador Frank McKenna (2005–6) put it: "Don't bring a knife to a gunfight." This means hiring lobbyists and lawyers to help us understand what is happening and complement our efforts. Intelligence garnered at the dinner table, the cocktail reception, at encounters on Capitol Hill, and from the administration is vital as both information and stock-in-trade. Ambassadors have always been equal parts saloon keeper, negotiator, and advocate, but they are also our interpreter, analyst, and chief intelligence officer.

We have a tendency to frame disputes as Canada versus the U.S. This works on the hockey rink, but in America it is a recipe for defeat and frustration. We always do better when we can make our issue a debate between Americans, when we can use their language and redefine it to our own ends.

—

3. *"All politics is local." It's a fifty-state campaign.*

Speaker Tip O'Neill's dictum "All politics is local," should be stenciled onto the cover of every Canadian briefing book. With elections every second year for the House of Representatives, politics is not just "all local" – it is "all retail." Unlike the Canadian system with its strict party discipline, Congress is like a game of tic-tac-toe – votes are traded based on personal connections and local interests. Most issues that become problems for us Canadian diplomats in Congress, particularly those that affect resources like lumber or products like steel, start at the state and local level. Once in Washington, there is momentum behind the issues and we end up playing defence.

Learn the lessons of American politics: it's a fifty-state campaign. Every strategy must have a micro-strategy, and tactics always vary. While Washington is the centre of American political life, the campaign field is all of America. Another way to look at the relationship is as a collection of sixty-three states and provinces operating under two federal frameworks. This web of networks – governments, business, labour, civil society, and the media – are like the interlocking rings in the Olympic logo. The personal relationships of governors and premiers are especially important and constitute the hidden wiring of the relationship. Cultivating these circles of influence and better coordinating these relationships is an ongoing requirement.

We've expanded our advocacy operation through our network of consulates that now extend into the American heartland. Our goal should be to situate a representative presence in every American state to listen, watch, and speak out for Canada.

4. Think big.

"Make no little plans; they have no magic to stir men's blood," advised Daniel Burnham, the great Chicago architect and builder. "Make big plans, aim high in hope and work." Americans like big ideas. It is much easier to get their attention when we "think big" as we did with the Free Trade Agreement and the Acid Rain Accord. We also need to think big and play on a big field if we are to make the necessary trade-offs. Traditional diplomacy eschews linkage politics, but that is exactly how American politics operates.

In recent years there was a Canadian tendency to play "small ball" and focus on what Secretary of State Condoleeza Rice would call the "condominium issues." We need to be bold and bring substance to the table by drawing from our own global network and the advantages that we should enjoy, for example, with our Chinese and Indian diasporas. When we take the initiative and get ahead of the curve we can play a key role in design and implementation, but when we sulk and complain and hang back we end up following standards already set.

Brian Mulroney, who understood the American game better than any recent prime minister, put it best: "The golden rule of Canada-U.S. relations is very simple. We can disagree without being disagreeable. The Americans are very important to us. We know they are, notwithstanding the differences, our best ally, our closest neighbour, our biggest customer. There is also a rule of global politics – Canada's influence in the world is measured to a significant degree by the extent to which we are perceived as having real influence in Washington."

5. It starts with trust and relationships.

Access depends on relationships. "The most important responsibility that a prime minister has on his schedule," observed Brian Mulroney at the recent Reagan centenary in February, 2011, "is the Canada-United States relationship. If you don't get that right, you're going to have problems. . . . The relationships [between prime ministers and presidents] are absolutely indispensable. If you don't have a friendly and constructive personal relationship with the president of the United States, nothing is going to happen."

Candour comes with confidence. The Washington game is all about networking. Derek Burney (Candian ambassador from 1989 to 1993) writes in his memoir, *Getting It Done,* that the first priority of the ambassador and his team is to know the players. We need relationships at every level because of the troupe of players that can affect our interests. It's also a permanent campaign because the troupe is constantly shifting, aligning, and realigning.

America is a remarkably egalitarian society. It does not stand on ceremony. On Capitol Hill, and at the State House, what you bring to the table in content and persuasion is more valuable' than the title on your card. Indeed, as they say in Washington, the longer the title, the less the importance. Opportunity depends on access. This means shoe leather and button-holing in the halls of Congress and state legislatures. The protocol for these meetings is simple: know your "ask," and "be brief, be forthright, be gone." Follow up with calls in their district and then, recommence.

6. Bring value to the table. Avoid the tendency to preach.

America's global burden of primacy makes for a big field but as Raymond Chrétien, Canadian ambassador from 1994 to 2000, observed in a speech in 1997, America's "national sense of self and singularity and global mission is a tremendous asset, but it can become self absorbing." If we are smart, Canadian diplomats can harness that self-absorption. Using intelligence from our own global diplomatic network, we can always find an angle of convergence that captures American attention. By reinforcing our credibility as serious players on issues that matter to America, we advance our own interests.

There is genuine interest in the White House, Pentagon, and State Department in new intelligence or a different perspective from their allies especially, as diplomat-scholar John Holmes observed in *Life with Uncle*, because Americans "need best friends to tell them when their breath is bad." Holmes defined this as the art of "alliancemanship." He also observed that the continuing challenge for Canadian leadership is to avoid "flippant disagreement" because we have "our own sour reputation for nauseous holiness and hypocrisy to cope with, our rhetoric outpacing our contribution."

7. Institutions and summitry work.

The great architect of European unity, Jean Monnet, once observed, "Nothing is possible without men, but nothing is lasting without institutions." Institutions, with their formal rules and conventions, act to level the playing field, and this is especially so when the relationship is asymmetrical. Summitry began with Mackenzie King and Calvin Coolidge meeting in Washington in 1927 to discuss trade and transportation issues, but it was the meetings on defence partnership and the economic relationship between Mackenzie King and Franklin Roosevelt in the lead up to and throughout the Second World War that set the model for future interaction between presidents and prime ministers. Summits are most effective when they are regular and results-oriented – winning a war or achieving a major objective, like the agreements on free trade and acid rain.

Arrangements that remind Americans of Canadian interests and provide a framework for discussion and dispute settlement are vital to Canadian interests. We've created hundreds of them – from the International Joint Commission to the Permanent Joint Board on Defence – and we should use them to maximum effect. Nor should we lose sight of the Gotliebian objective of a "community of law" whereby the rule of law would replace political discretion by either government, and, as really matters to Canada, the exercise of raw political power.

8. Team Canada, Inc.

For Gotlieb, it was the "multipicity of instruments." For Frank McKenna, it was the "thousand points of contact." Both understood the importance of using all of our assets in a Team Canada, Inc. approach: sing from the same hymnal, but in different places and using different voices to break through the chaotic cacophony that is the American system in the age of the Internet.

Most business interactions between Canada and the U.S. take place with minimal government involvement. Yet corporate involvement is vital. Planning and investment are measured in decades rather than election cycles because corporations want regulatory constancy. Businesses will engage in policy development as long as it is results oriented. The corporate world has little patience for "consultations" that seem to be political posturing or window dressing. We need to develop a permanent public-private advisory council that governments, federal and provincial, can turn to for advice and rely on for support and advocacy.

Labour also needs to be brought into planning and discussions early. A third of Canadian unions are affiliates of their American brethren, yet this relationship is too often under-utilized, especially when dealing with the perennial problem of "Buy America." Unions are a vital component of the Democratic coalition: they contribute volunteers and money, which gives them an active voice at the leadership tables in Congress and the White House. For example, the Canadian Steelworkers played a lead role in securing exemption from U.S. action aimed at European steelworkers in the early nineties, and Ambassador Doer called on union support during the successful negotiations leading to the U.S.-Canada Government Procurement Agreement (February 16, 2010).

9. It's a permanent campaign.

As long as there is an interest group with a gripe and the ear of its congressional representatives, we need to be engaged. Massachusetts timber merchants, in what is now Maine, persuaded the George Washington administration in the first year of its first term in 1789 to impose a five-per-cent tariff on imports of New Brunswick timber. Since then the U.S. has imposed restrictions on Canadian lumber imports more than thirty times.

We need to be in a permanent campaign in defence of our interests. More than half a century ago, Ambassador Hume Wrong observed in a 1951 dispatch home that "we rightly distrust the processes whereby American foreign policy is influenced from day to day and are never sure of its steadiness and consistency," and this still hasn't changed. It means doing diplomacy differently with a premium on public diplomacy and rapid response and using all of our assets – embassy, business, lobbyists, lawyers, and legislators at the federal, provincial, and municipal levels. Nor, as Ambassador Frank McKenna observed in 2005, is it ever over: "If and when this case is resolved – don't stop. You must permanently protect your interests."

10. Tend the garden.

Relationships, former Secretary of State George Shultz has observed on numerous occasions, are like gardens. They need constant care and weeding. The more complex the garden, the more attention is required, and what worked in one season may not work in the next. So it is with the Canada-U.S. partnership. The current U.S. ambassador, David Jacobson, has remarked that, "You Canadians think you know all about us. We Americans think we know all we need to know about you. We're both wrong."

But Canada can't afford to get it wrong. We need to understand America and its idiosyncrasies. Our destiny remains tied to our geography. In terms of Canadian interests, the

Gotlieb precept continues to hold true: there is the United States . . . then there is the rest. The conditions and actors change, but the game and its goal – advancing Canadian interests – remains the same.

DEFYING GRAVITY:
Canada's Search for Counterweights to the United States

Brian Bow

The United States is going through hard times again, and once again this has triggered a debate in Canada about whether to hold on tighter or to seek greener pastures abroad, perhaps in rapidly growing economies like China, India, or Brazil. This debate is a familiar one in small and middle-sized countries, but no country experiences it in the all-consuming, existential way that Canada does, because no country is as wedged in, geographically, as Canada is. Our unique place in the world, spread out alongside and culturally attuned to the world's most powerful and economically dynamic country, and separated from the rest of the world by vast stretches of cold water, has made us very cozy with the U.S., but has also "trapped" us with the U.S. – at least in economic terms. Yet some of us wonder whether, in this age of globalization, geography matters less than it once did, freeing us to choose new international partners, and to sink or swim as genuinely global players.

We have faced this kind of choice before, but we haven't always made the same decision. In the 1970s, when the U.S. was down and we were on the outs with them, the Trudeau government sought "counterweights," by reaching out to Europe and Japan. In the 1980s, when the U.S. was suffering a recession and we worried that its markets were closing to our products, the Mulroney government chose to cling more tightly to the U.S. Today, facing the same dilemma, we see again the same kinds of arguments being made, but this time we cannot seem to make up our minds.

Here I will offer a very brief overview of the history of this debate, and try to uncover the reasons why we have tilted one way or the other, with the hope that this might shed new light on the choices we face today. I argue that in the past our choices have been affected by four main factors: Canada's sense of national self-confidence, moral evaluations of the United States and its policies, the ideological and practical compatibility of national leaders' agendas, and rhetorical pushing and pulling by policy advocates. It seems today that the first three factors do not point decisively in either direction, and the fourth factor must eventually carry the day.

It's worth noting, to begin, that the current angst about our relationship with the U.S. is similar to the mixed feelings Canadians used to have about their ties to Britain. In the first half of the twentieth century, as Britain seemed to lose its footing as a global power, Canadians were torn about whether to try to tighten their relationship to the empire, or to break away and seek closer ties with the United States. (In fact, many of the recurring themes in Canada's late-twentieth-century anti-Americanism came out of earlier debates about why Canada ought to stick with "Mother England.") There were, moreover, many in the early twentieth century who argued Canada should try to make relations with the U.S. complement and support established ties to Britain and the Commonwealth by serving as a "bridge" between the old global hegemon and the new. But after

World War II, with the U.S. riding so high and Britain fallen so low, the choice was an easy one to make, and Canada jumped with both feet. And, as John English points out, the transition turned out to be a remarkably easy one, as the U.S. sought to win support and reassure allies by entangling itself in a network of multilateral institutions, and gave Canada an even better deal, through a series of special understandings and exemptions.[1]

In the early 1970s the Vietnam War, a worsening balance of payments, and domestic upheaval raised serious questions about whether the U.S. was in decline, perhaps even on the road to disaster. It was the "Nixon shocks" of August 1971, though, and the dispiriting struggle to get some kind of exemption from these new trade and investment restrictions, that brought on a "national catharsis" in Canada.[2] For many Canadians, this sense of crisis went beyond specific policy differences, raising doubts about whether Canada and the U.S. really "belonged together," and prompting some to think about finding "counterweights" abroad. This impulse was stirred by external pressures during that period, including: détente; decolonization; rapid growth in Europe and Japan; and the earliest manifestations of economic globalization, which made it cheaper to shift production and investment from one place to another. But it was domestic pressures that prompted the Trudeau government to act on that impulse: the public's desire to morally distance itself from the U.S. over the Vietnam War; the growth of nationalist sentiments; growing anxiety about foreign direct investment; the Liberals' growing interest in a more ambitious, interventionist federal government; and Trudeau's personal interest in Asia and the developing world.

The "Third Option" was unveiled in 1972 as a plan to strengthen Canada's control over its own destiny by empowering the federal government and seeking new diplomatic and commercial partners abroad. A "contractual link" was negotiated with the European Community, new overtures were made to Japan, and there were expressions of solidarity and support for the developing world. But the contractual link came to virtually nothing. Japan was indifferent to Canada's advances, and Canada – like the other advanced, industrial economies – rejected the Group of 77's call for a restructuring of the world economy. There were no obvious bases for diplomatic and economic breakthroughs with these new partners, and, even with the federal government beating the bushes for new trade deals, Canadian businesses showed little interest in moving on from the familiar U.S. market to challenging new environments overseas. The Third Option was never meant to fundamentally reorient Canadian foreign policy, but its supposed failure to do so had a profound effect on the attentive public's perceptions of what was possible, effectively limiting the debate to two options, at least for a while.[3]

It was no surprise, then, that when things got tough again for the United States in the early 1980s, Canada made very different choices. The U.S. was hit by a deep recession in 1981, which quickly spread to Canada and beyond. Germany and Japan, however, continued to grow rapidly, and many worried that the U.S. and its basic economic model were being eclipsed. This apprehension was picked up on in Ottawa, but it did not have much of an impact on Canadian strategy debates. The overriding concern in Canada was the wave of protectionism triggered in the U.S. by the recession, and the concern that Canadian producers were losing access to the all-important American market. Thus, rather than debating the merits of seeking out new markets overseas, Canadian policy-makers very quickly agreed that their top priority must be to protect its existing footholds in the U.S. market, and to build up Canada's global competitiveness by reducing barriers to trade and investment with the U.S. Whereas in the 1970s there had been an active debate, with some arguing against the "counterweights" strategy, in the 1980s there was a virtual consensus around focusing on renewing ties with the U.S.[4]

Again, external pressures played an important role in shaping Canada's choice: the "return" of the Cold War and renewed pressures for alliance cohesion; falling world prices for commodity exports like oil; and, most importantly, the Reagan administration's schizophrenic mixture of free-market liberalism (in theory) and recession-induced protectionism (in practice). And again, internal pressures were probably decisive, mostly in terms of lessons learned from the Trudeau years: that the counterweights strategy could not work, and that state intervention to redirect the market led only to economic and political trouble. Looking back on it now, it is clear that the cementing of this worldview in the 1980s had much to do with Mulroney's ideological commitments and his desire to tear down Trudeau's legacy. But the story is more complicated than that, because the reorientation actually began under Trudeau, with the "de-fanging" of the Foreign Investment Review Act and the Macdonald Commission's recommendation to negotiate sectoral trade liberalization. Given the supposed failure of the Third Option, the intensity of the political backlash triggered by the National Energy

Program, and the broader shift toward free-market strategies throughout the developed economies in the 1980s and 1990s, it should not be surprising that both Conservatives and Liberals were now more skeptical about state-led efforts to redirect international economic relationships.

In the 1990s there was another push to build new economic relationships abroad in the Chrétien government's courting of the Asia-Pacific world. This effort was very different from the two previous ones, however, because it came out of very different circumstances. Whereas in the 1970s and 1980s, the U.S. was widely seen to be suffering relative decline; in the 1990s it was on a roll, having just "won" the Cold War, and then – after a brief downturn in 1990–91 – going through a period of sustained growth, while Germany and (later) Japan were struggling. And whereas in the 1970s Canadians were talking about going into Asia *instead* of the U.S., in the 1990s they were going into Asia *alongside* the U.S., chasing the same trade and investment opportunities that seemed to be erupting all over the region. There was some talk during this period about a historic shift of power from West to East, but Canada's push into the region seemed to be driven mainly by the expectation of short- and medium-term profits. While many new commercial connections were made in Asia, there were far fewer than many had hoped, and most evaporated when the Asian financial crisis hit in 1997. From the point of view of today's debates, this was important mostly because it helped to reinforce skepticism in Canadian government and business circles about the prospects for building important new relationships overseas, whether under the rubric of a search for counterweights or not. There was a lot of excitement in Ottawa about catching the Asia-Pacific wave, but in practice Canadians continued to find it easier and ultimately more rewarding to stick with what was familiar – the United States.

The 2000s were strikingly similar in some ways to the 1970s. The U.S. was seen to have been humbled by misguided foreign policy decisions, torn by domestic upheaval, and weakened by economic setbacks, which ran out of control after 2008, opening the door to emerging rivals like China and India. As in the 1970s and 1980s, there were profound tensions within the transatlantic alliance, and the U.S. seemed to have lost its authority to lead. Again there was talk of a restructuring of the global order, and perhaps of global institutions to fit that new order, which had Canada (rightly) frightened that it might lose its place in the club of major international players. And, more immediately, there was again a deep anxiety about the security of Canada's access to the U.S. market, this time because of the tightening of the border after 9/11.

Today there is no consensus about how Canada should position itself within this very challenging global environment. Some, echoing the "counterweights" arguments of the early 1970s, have argued that we must accept and adapt to the United States's decline by building up new relationships with rising powers like China and India. Others have argued that while there is no doubt that other powers are rising, the U.S. is not in danger of going down the tubes, and Canadians cannot afford to get distracted from the all-important task of rebuilding the bilateral relationship with our neighbour to the south. And a third group – probably the largest one – has argued that the two strategies can be reconciled, by going out into the wider world to build new relationships, but doing so in a way that reaffirms and supports our bilateral relationship with the United States.

There are four factors – as noted – that, in the past, have determined which way Canada will tilt on this question. First, in times when Canadians' national self-confidence is high, as in the early 1970s, they may be inclined to take a more "independent" posture, and to seek out new partners abroad. When it comes to the economy, our experiences in the 1970s and 1980s suggest that this sense of self-confidence is apparently not tied to overall economic growth, but rather to commodity prices, which have much to do with our prospects for breaking into new markets abroad and drawing in desirable new investments at home. The picture today is mixed because Canadians are worried about the deterioration of their profile and influence in the world (shrinking military and aid budgets, failed bid for a UN Security Council seat, etc.), but they take some comfort (probably too much)[5] in the way they have carried on through the ongoing global economic crisis.

Second, in times when Canadians strongly object to American leaders and policies, they have a strong impulse to distance themselves from the U.S. both morally and practically, and may do so by seeking out new partners. George W. Bush was reviled by many in Canada, and that contempt and mistrust fueled the perception – in some parts of Canada – that the U.S. was declining, that Canada had more in common with Europeans than with Americans, and that standing "shoulder to shoulder" with the U.S. might seriously undercut our prospects for friendly relations with others. Barack Obama, on the other hand, is much more popular in Canada, and has remained so even while his popularity declines in the

United States; the recent resuscitation of "security perimeter" talks suggests that Canadians are much happier to get closer to the U.S. while Obama is president than they were with Bush.[6] But the financial crisis and resulting recession have soured many Canadians on the American system and reinforced the argument that it is dangerous to be too tightly tied to the U.S. economy.

Third, in times when the prime minister's and the president's foreign and domestic policy agendas are in conflict, it is more likely that policy makers in Canada will want to seek new international allies in order to accomplish their goals. Harper and Obama have different personal priorities on issues like climate change, the Israel-Palestine conflict, and relations with China. But these differences have not come to a head because Obama has been held back by domestic obstacles, and is likely to be even more tied up for the remainder of this term, as the Republican majority forces him to make budget cuts and challenges his international agreements.

These first three factors, taken together, do not really point us in one direction or another. Thus there is real space today for the fourth factor to come to the fore, as policy entrepreneurs (inside and outside of government) seek to define the options and build consensus around a favoured strategy.

If any group has momentum now, then it is those who argue for finding a way to combine building new relationships overseas with renewing the bilateral relationship with the U.S. The Canadian International Council's recently published *Open Canada* report, for example, argues that "we must *deepen* our U.S. connections while we *broaden* our economic portfolio away from reliance on a single market."[7] It makes sense, intuitively, that Canadians would want to have their cake and eat it too. And it's not surprising that this impulse would be stronger now, in light of the lessons learned from the 1970s and 1980s. With one prime minister taken to task for quixotically chasing counterweights and another criticized for getting too close to the Americans, the overall lesson seems to be that one cannot be seen to tilt too far one way or the other. But do we really have the option to do both? Is that really a coherent strategy?

Many arguments for a synergistic strategy are hopelessly vague about what it might look like in practice. But some have specific tactics in mind, which we can assess more concretely. Some advocate that Canada try to earn goodwill in the EU and the U.S. simultaneously, by brokering a deal on troop contributions in Afghanistan, or on climate change. The *Open Canada* report argued that we should pursue closer relations with Mexico and other Latin American states, partly to serve Canada's economic and security interests directly, but also to support the U.S. agenda in the region, and thereby strengthen Canada-U.S. relations.[8] Wendy Dobson and Diana Kuzmanovic have argued that Canada can get greater leverage with the U.S. by "deepen[ing] NAFTA" through participation in the Trans-Pacific Partnership trade regime.[9]

These arguments often do point to specific synergies, many of which should be pursued. But they do not necessarily amount to an across-the-board strategy to guide Canadian foreign policy choices. The fact is that we will sometimes be forced, just as we have been in the past, to choose between pleasing the U.S. and pleasing other (potential or actual) partners overseas. Should we create tax and subsidy incentives to encourage Canadian producers out into the wider world or to encourage foreign investors into the Canadian market, even if that provokes indignation in Washington (and legal challenges through the World Trade Organization)? Should we welcome Chinese investments in the Alberta oil sands? Should our relations with India be driven by commercial opportunities, or should we use trade ties to try to influence their relations with Pakistan and Afghanistan? And when tensions are high between the U.S. and the Europeans, who should we support on issues like climate change, Israel-Palestine, or NATO burden-sharing?

It is important here to separate the political arena from the policy-making world. In the political arena, arguments about overarching foreign policy strategies are important, if only in constructing a coherent narrative about the party's overall "philosophy" for foreign policy. In the policy-making world, however, these debates are not taken seriously, in day-to-day decision making or in long-term policy planning. The questions raised here are important ones, but they are not necessarily connected, and need not be deliberately linked. The question for the policy maker in Ottawa is not whether it is the U.S. or China that is more important to Canada, but rather what can be done to maximize our overall gains in our day-to-day dealings with each. And decisions about which opportunities to pursue are made according to the balance of benefits and costs for each specific foreign policy move, according to the policy makers' own assessments of national interest, but always with an eye on the anticipated public reaction. It is this last element that brings us full circle, to the place where the political arena and the policy-making world intersect, as ivory tower and campaign trail debates about big strategic-orientation concepts – for example, continentalism versus counterweights versus combination – ultimately do shape the general public's thinking about what our choices are, and what priorities ought to guide those choices.

I expect Canada's overall approach to foreign policy in the 2010s to be a mash-up of greatest hits from previous decades, both in rhetoric and in practice. From the 1970s (and the 2000s) there will be much talk about the inevitability of U.S. relative decline, and the growing urgency of seeking out new partners abroad. But these will probably be free of the kind of naive arguments about a fundamental reorientation of our diplomacy and trade that were common in the 1970s. From the 1980s, there will be continuing anxiety about the need to restore our relationship with the U.S. – particularly our access to the American market – and many new proposals to do so by negotiating integrative bilateral agreements and institutions. But only a few will be making the arguments that the state has no role to play in guiding economic choices, or that paying attention to other countries is always a distraction from our "main game." There will also be extensive borrowing from the 1990s, in the sense that our pursuit of new diplomatic and commercial partners in other regions will most likely continue to be opportunistic, ad hoc, and generally not very ambitious, in the way that Chrétien's Asia-Pacific campaign was. (Most of the business community in Canada is, after all, still "singularly ill prepared to deal with [the business] environment [in Asia], especially as traders."[10]) But of course no one in government will talk about the policy this way, while strong proponents of closer relations with China, India, and other rising powers will continue to complain about Canada's half-hearted, "day-tripper" approach.

Taken together, these elements will add up to a rather "unstrategic" approach, which seeks to make gains in the U.S. and with rising powers at the same time, and just crosses its fingers that no zero-sum choices come along. None of our foreign policy visionaries will like it very much, but it just might be the best available option.

Notes

1   John English, "Canada in the Post-American World," in Sean Clark and Sabrina Hoque, eds., *Debating a Post-American World: What Lies Ahead?* (New York: Routledge, forthcoming).

2   Peter C. Dobell, "Reducing Vulnerability: The Third Option, 1970s," in Don Munton and John Kirton, *Canadian Foreign Policy: Selected Cases* (Toronto: Prentice Hall, 1992), 237.

3   Gordon Mace and Gérard Hervouet, "Canada's Third Option: A Complete Failure?" *Canadian Public Policy* 15 no. 4 (December 1989): 387–404.

4   Brian Bow, "Unstoppable Force or Immovable Object?: Crisis and the Social Construction of North America," in Jeffrey Ayres and Laura Macdonald, eds., *North America in Question: Regional Integration in an Era of Political Economic Turbulence* (Toronto: University of Toronto Press, 2011).

5   Barrie McKenna, "'Stunning Loss' of Canadian Market Share in the US," *Globe and Mail*, December 17, 2010.

6   Lawrence Martin, "Open Minds, Open Borders," *Globe and Mail*, February 8, 2011.

7   Canadian International Council (CIC), *Open Canada: A Global Positioning Strategy for a Networked Age*, June 2010, 20.

8   CIC, *Open Canada*, 51–5.

9   Wendy Dobson and Diana Kuzmanovic, "Differentiating Canada: The Future of the Canada-U.S. Relationship," *University of Calgary School of Public Policy Research Papers* 3 no. 7 (November 2010).

10   Donald S. Macdonald, "Three Perspectives on Canada's Future," *Daedalus* 117 no. 4 (Fall 1988): 363–80, 367–8.

CANADA, THE U.S., NORTH AMERICA, AND THE WORLD

Jeremy Kinsman

Why were Allan Gotlieb's influence and reach as ambassador to Washington in the 1980s exceptional – in fact, unique? On the Washington "sexy issues" list, Canada's interests when he arrived were, as usual, policy wallflowers, gazing longingly at the attention others attracted. How did a bookish, intellectual, government-service lifer move Canada to the centre of the dance floor? The answer is not a no-brainer. Gotlieb did it with intellect, not a feature valued in Canada's less creative, less permissive, and much less effective political and public service culture today.

Allan Gotlieb received a boost not long after arriving in Washington in the fall of 1981, when his writer wife Sondra penetrated the *Washington Post*'s op-ed circle with a weekly faux-naïf, satirical column about Washingtonians' main interest, namely themselves. Senators who hadn't given Canada a moment's thought loved the *Post* tickling their own Vanity Fair, and became suckers for invitations to the gala parties the Gotliebs launched in a town that was shucking off the cloth coats of the Carter years.

Obviously, however, Gotlieb's influence wasn't mainly that of a party giver. It came from his commitment to the power of ideas. The example his time in Washington provides for the present is that we need to valorize ideas again, for both international and North American affairs, and empower people with communications and policy capabilities to advance them in Washington and in the U.S. public policy community.

(Author's disclosure: Allan Gotlieb was a generous boss, mentor, and friend in those days thirty years ago. In the first rating report he wrote of me, he noted approvingly that I "kept up with scholarly journals," an unusual observation in the public service. In truth, I hadn't. But I have ever since.)

A critical perception of Gotlieb's was related to the notorious maxim of House Speaker Tip O'Neill that "all politics is local." Gotlieb grasped that Canadian interests in Washington were inextricably bound up in U.S. domestic politics. In both Ottawa and Washington, Canada-U.S. bilateral issues were handled as foreign policy issues. But in the U.S. political sausage factory, the protection of U.S. ranchers, lumber mills, and carbon dioxide–spewing power plants was decidedly local.

Public diplomacy protagonism, Gotlieb-style, was launched a month after his arrival. He gave a speech in New York heavily criticizing a protectionist trade reciprocity bill in Congress that was already supported by the administration. Beyond the usual complaint that it would hurt Canada, he spelled out how it would unravel the General Agreement on Tariffs and Trade (GATT) where deals were cross-sectoral, and how it would generally damage both the world and the U.S. economies.

Ottawa officials were horrified that the ambassador loudly attacked Congress and the administration, in public, over pending legislation. His analysis made the front pages of the

New York Times and the *Washington Post*. The embassy had five hundred requests for copies from staffers on the Hill. Not long after, U.S. Special Trade Representative Bill Brock reversed the administration's position and killed the bill, using portions of Gotlieb's big-picture speech to explain why.

That speech succeeded because it was an argument of ideas, and it linked Canadian insight on world issues to a specific measure of domestic U.S. politics.

Gotlieb knew Canada's lack of political capital in Washington meant we had to compete at the level of ideas. To be listened to, he needed the stature of a go-to guy who could illuminate the issues Washington took most seriously. He addressed world issues high on the U.S. agenda by drawing from a useful Canadian perspective and record. His development of intellectual analyses of the issues earned him access, and influence, to deploy in support of mutual objectives. On bilateral issues, he connected the dots for Americans who couldn't see the bigger picture regarding Canada, and helped Canadians understand the U.S. system. In doing so, he generated solutions.

What Gotlieb did on a personal level, Canada needs to do today at the policy level – connect to the U.S. political leadership, including President Obama, by fishing out our old calling card as a high-performance, high-conviction world player.

Doing more than one thing at a time

Over the years, Canadian "continentalist" circles held our bilateral issues with the U.S. to be just about all the foreign policy content we needed. Other ambitions and activity on the world stage were seen as distractions from what was vital, and as potential complications in our life with Washington.

If such a self-limiting position stood up for the sake of argument when Canadian merchandise exports to a booming U.S. reached 87 per cent of our total ("Only thirteen to go," one wag in the Pearson Building teased), it is without legs today as that percentage sinks to the low seventies. It also completely misses the fact that in other markets, especially the EU, very significant Canadian foreign investment creates business, not merchandise exports. We trade *in* those markets more than *to* them.

Worries about being tied to a wobbly U.S. economy and financial picture have persuaded some commentators, such as Jeffrey Simpson of the *Globe and Mail*, that we must (among other things) refocus on diversifying our economy outside North America. Canada needs to make its mark within the new global distribution of power and influence. But at the same time, geography, political reality, our livelihoods, and a more or less common culture keep North America as the continental home base where we *must* succeed. Continentally, knowing the deadlocked U.S. political process inhibits long-term strategic thinking, some U.S. officials have encouraged Canadian partners to take the initiative to propose big-picture ways to enhance cooperation in the North American neighbourhood, including on global issues such as the climate-change-and-energy swirl, where North America working together might become a global "first mover."

Internationally, the WikiLeaks cables depict U.S. representatives abroad as often working alone on peace and security issues, against a wave of almost ubiquitous corruption and political double-dealing. The Obama administration would welcome a North American partner active in the world, able to bring to bear on key issues the specialty ideas and action-edge of a wide-ranging democratic middle power.

Are we up to it?

Connecting and counting at the policy level

In what areas can Canada lend a hand? Do we have influence in any of them? Afghanistan, of course, stands out as a place where Canada has made an outsized contribution. Mexico ought to, as well, but Canadians have ducked engagement there in recent years, reluctant to participate in tripartite issues for fear our one-on-one relationship with the U.S. will suffer.

Allan Gotlieb worries today that despite hints from Washington we should push the North American envelope, Americans have little strategic appreciation of Canada itself. We should be front and centre of American strategic thinking, as the nation's biggest neighbour, customer, and supplier of the national drug – energy – but we aren't.

When President Obama's nominee as ambassador to Canada went before the Senate subcommittee, no senators showed up. The lame-duck appointee to Vice President Biden's old seat in Delaware had to be catapulted in to get a quorum of one senator. But at hearings for the nominee for ambassador to Mexico, senators not even on the committee competed to pile in as guests.

Over twenty million Hispanic voters in the U.S. constitute an obvious political reality. Mexican democracy is battling narco-traffickers ominously connected to the U.S. drug market. Such facts and worries, as well as a century and a half of legendary conflict with Mexico, explain why from Washington, Mexico City looks like a capital of vital interest and Ottawa seems a backwater.

In terms of foreign policy, Canada needs to play up our credentials as a smaller, reliable, developed democracy with a long-standing record in multilateral creativity, especially useful in the very peace, security, and arms control creative work that the U.S., as a superpower, can't lead on. It means reviving the quality of the personal relationships Canadian leaders once had around the world, ones that can assist in conflict mediation (as the Norwegians have done) and in global cooperation.

Continentally, it calls for connecting to U.S. interests (including in supporting Mexico) by advancing proposals to shore up North America. Bilaterally, it doesn't mean avoiding disagreements with the U.S. by downplaying differences; it means situating them, as Gotlieb did, in a larger, dot-connected, positive context.

Gotlieb and Trudeau

Allan Gotlieb came to Washington in the autumn of 1981 very much as Pierre Trudeau's ambassador. Trudeau saw in Gotlieb an intellectual companionship, and Trudeau needed a sharp mind in Washington. He had little personal feeling for or experience with the U.S. or its culture, political or otherwise. (Picture this: 1983, Prime Minister Trudeau on a visit to Washington to see Reagan. A big dinner party scheduled at the residence is delayed an hour because Reagan, on a day's notice, must address a special session of Congress about Central America. So, waiting guests, including the prime minister, watch Reagan's speech on TV. Trudeau turns to fellow guests Donald Sutherland and Christopher Plummer – Canadian celebrity artists at embassy dinners being another Gotlieb-era innovation – and says "What communications skills! He's a genius!" Apparently, the prime minister had never seen the president at the podium before. The two veteran actors scoffed: "Are you kidding, Prime Minister? That's what actors *do*.")

Bilaterally, the hand of cards Gotlieb had to play was quasi-adversarial, dealt by Canada's phase of economic nationalism that followed Richard Nixon's sudden unilateral surcharge on U.S. imports a decade earlier. This "Nixon shock" led to the "Third Option," the Trudeau government's adoption of a variety of defensive and strategic interventionist economic instruments such as Foreign Investment Revue Agency (FIRA), the Canada Development Corporation (CDC), Petro-Canada, and ultimately the National Energy Program (NEP) to "reduce the current vulnerability" to arbitrary U.S. decisions.

After Nixon's political fall, Trudeau developed a close intellectual relationship with Jimmy Carter. Trudeau's preoccupations with North-South disparities, the vast number of nuclear weapons in the hands of the superpowers, and the dangers of nuclear proliferation, earned him influence and, indirectly, Carter's support for Canadian unity at a very challenging time.

Carter's presidency perished in the sand in Iran. Détente was crushed by the Soviet invasion of Afghanistan. Challenged for much of his term by deep recession, staggering oil prices, and startling inflation, he spoke hard truths to existentially optimistic Americans who recoiled at being nagged that they suffered from a "malaise."

Ronald Reagan made them feel good again. The current centenary of Ronald Reagan's birth has propelled his reputation skyward in a glow of nostalgia, but at the time he was, internationally, a polarizing political figure whose hardline views on global issues Trudeau cared most about (détente and North-South disparities) aroused antipathy and caricature both abroad and in Canada. Meanwhile, Canada's "nationalist" economic policies annoyed the Reagan administration.

Reagan's people didn't put Trudeau on a Nixonian list of enemies, but they distrusted his exotic intellectualism. On the other hand, they did concede he was a world player connected to a wide range of leaders like Olof Palme, Andreas Papandreou, Julius Nyerere, François Mitterrand, Helmut Schmidt, and Lee Kuan Yew.

Trudeau had chaired the G-7 Summit in Montebello in July, 1981, where he aimed to introduce the North-South theme of "power-sharing" (which in a way foretold the world landscape today). Reagan's election in November undermined the initiative's chances, but Trudeau insisted G-7 leaders spend half a day on the theme, despite the new president's indifference and active skepticism from Mrs Thatcher. In October, 1981, Trudeau again pursued the North-South power-sharing theme as co-chair of a summit of twenty-two world leaders in Cancun, Mexico. It enabled the newly minted Ambassador Gotlieb, who had organized the Montebello Summit, to interpret Trudeau and his ideas to Washington officials and journalists. The ambassador was in the public eye, where an effective ambassador ought to be.

Celebrity-susceptible America (and everywhere else) had more interest in Trudeau than in any Canadian prime minister before or since. This interest helped Gotlieb present Canada across the U.S. to countless chapters of the World Affairs Council, the UN Association, and other citizens' and business groups. Gotlieb tried to mobilize such pockets of sympathy in favour of Canada's nation building at home. Not many Americans bought in to the idea of a squeeze on access to Canadian oil under the NEP, but public diplomacy did help on the acid rain files. Canada had many natural allies, if not in the lions' dens of the smoke-stacked Midwest, most assuredly in New England and California, when it came to addressing the effects of industrial pollution.

In the 1980s, Canada's role as a worrier about Cold War antagonisms stood for many internationalist Americans as an intelligent contrast to the ideological and unilateralist assertiveness they heard from Reagan's Washington.

After nervous Soviet defenders shot down straying Korean Air Lines Flight 007 in the fall of 1983, background intelligence showed U.S. spokesmen lied when they said they had "proof" the U.S.S.R. knew they were shooting down a civilian airliner. Alarmed that such tactics heightened nuclear risk, Trudeau mounted a global "peace initiative" aimed at resetting some of the nuclear rules. It sat badly in Washington, which felt that when Trudeau talked about U.S.-U.S.S.R. nuclear build-down (as opposed to non-proliferation, where Canada had earned some credibility), he was out of his non-nuclear league and was essentially interfering.

But Reagan listened when, after a briefing by Gotlieb, Trudeau urged him to make his destiny as a man of peace who could break the nuclear arsenals down – which is what eventually happened at the Reagan-Gorbachev Summit in 1986.

Gotlieb has written that Trudeau over-reached and erred in challenging Reagan (and Thatcher) at successive G-7 and NATO summits. Trudeau's contrarian impulses did irritate Reagan aides, protective of their often simplifying but, to them, inspiring president. They were used to running world affairs as they saw fit.

Gotlieb believed Canada should have cooled its differences with Reagan when we needed U.S. cooperation on vital bilateral files. Much later, he proposed that Canadian policy had to resist "romantic" impulses for internationalist engagement if they came at a cost to relations with the U.S., which, as a "realist," he had to place at the top of any Canadian priority list. He argued that a demonstrably more harmonious working relationship with Washington would likely impress the world to Canada's benefit more than initiatives undertaken independently.

The counterpoint is that Trudeau's determination to stand up to Washington won Canada increased political standing elsewhere in the world, though not with Mrs. Thatcher, who anyway believed the most special relationship the U.S. had was with Britain. During U.S. administrations that are globally abrasive, such as that of President Bush Jr, Canada is often looked to as "the other North America" in a positive sense. But there is a political price to pay in Washington for the Canadian leader who talks down the U.S. abroad just to score points with others or to win votes at home (as Paul Martin did in his 2006 campaign). It would need another Canadian prime minister to try to reset the mixture. Gotlieb saw the opportunity in the election of Brian Mulroney.

The Mulroney years

Brian Mulroney and Ronald Reagan's privileged personal relationship enabled Canada to settle the acid rain file and eventually enter into free trade negotiations. (Even detailed accounts of the Canada-U.S. Free Trade Agreement negotiation saga generally omit the narrative of how the Mulroney government, as urged by Allan Gotlieb, became Canada's most beneficial ever to arts and culture in order to assuage anxieties over assimilation and national identity in English Canada. Canadian identity has never been more robust than it is today.)

Reagan's persona as the Cold Warrior ("Mr. Gorbachev, tear down this wall!") would be re-cast by the rapidly changing relationship with the new and radically different Soviet leader. Keeping Canada's view in the game, Gotlieb had arranged for recently retired Canadian ambassador to Moscow, Robert Ford, to come to Washington to brief Secretary of State George Shultz on developments.

Ford was an initial skeptic about the authenticity of glasnost and perestroika. But Brian Mulroney was ahead of the curve, building outstanding relationships with Gorbachev and then with Boris Yeltsin. At G-7 and other summits, Mulroney argued for taking Gorbachev's initiatives seriously, and also insisted on forcing an end to apartheid in South Africa. Mrs. Thatcher held out on both counts, but Reagan shifted positions, and eventually the British prime minister came around.

Once Vice President Bush won the presidency in 1988, in what was becoming a dramatically changed world, the much more nuanced and multilateralist instincts of the new administration matched Canadian internationalist DNA.

Mulroney's ties in both Commonwealth and francophone circles reverberated in Washington. Canada's role in diplomacy and hard power came through on the United Nations Security Council, which set up the massive international expeditionary force to throw Iraq out of Kuwait. Reflecting Canada's political clout, President Bush favoured Mulroney as secretary-general of the UN. Some years later, then–Secretary of State James Baker recalled the relationship (for an Oxford-Princeton audience) as one in which "We could always count on Canada to do the right thing."

The Bush-Mulroney years represented an exceptional period of creative harmony in both substance and mood, when ideas were at the fore of foreign policy. It was, in many ways, the relationship Gotlieb had aimed for, though his own stewardship in Washington ended in 1988 after seven years. Harmony relied, of course, on the U.S. administration itself also "doing the right thing," which would not always be the case.

The Clinton-Chrétien era

If Brian Mulroney had ridden into power charging that Pierre Trudeau had been too distant from Washington, Jean Chrétien, in return, charged Mulroney with being too near. So it goes.

But Chrétien developed an unusually close friendship with Bill Clinton that served Canada well when Clinton gave unstinting support to Canadian unity at the time of the second Quebec referendum. Bilateral disagreements were relatively few.

On foreign policy, the capitals were in sync. Chrétien was a global player who enjoyed wide-ranging personal ties with leaders such as Fernando Henrique Cardoso of Brazil, Ernesto Zedillo of Mexico, Romano Prodi of Italy, Boris Yeltsin, and Jacques Chirac. These counted to Canada's credit in international meetings and also in Washington. Chrétien's political smarts were respected internationally, in part for the gut instincts Canadians knew, but also for his ability to do in his own way what Gotlieb had recommended – grasp a partner's interests and make common cause.

A surge in Canada's international profile occurred when Lloyd Axworthy took over Foreign Affairs and launched Canada's "human security agenda" with support from Britain's New Labour Party. Inventive alliances with international civil society challenged log-jams of especially military conservatism on such issues as the International Criminal Court, the Land Mines Convention, and child soldiers. After Srebrenica and Rwanda, the "responsibility to protect" initiative dented the UN doctrine that cherished the supremacy of non-interference in internal affairs.

Lloyd Axworthy kept a friendly channel open with Secretary of State Madeleine Albright. Nevertheless, the U.S. didn't sign on to the International Criminal Court (ICC) or the Land Mines Convention. The election of George W. Bush in 2000 made sure they wouldn't.

The post–9/11 years

In terms of Canada-U.S. relations, these were the "years the locusts ate." September 11 turned America into a fortress behind a thickened border that had seemed almost non-existent under NAFTA. U.S. Ambassador Paul Cellucci scolded that "security trumps trade," thereby upending Canadian assumptions about the relationship.

Initial limited NATO deployments to Afghanistan, moved by Canada in the North Atlantic Council, showed a spirit of solidarity and an almost existential commitment for the UN-authorized mission in response to the 9/11 attacks. This contrasted to later Canadian aversion to what it saw as the careening of the Bush administration, with Tony Blair's seemingly inexplicable support, toward the regime-change invasion of Iraq, which essentially permitted the Taliban to return to Afghanistan.

In 2003, Jean Chrétien gave way to Paul Martin, who soon committed Canadian Forces to Kandahar, where there would be a level of violence the Canadian military had not anticipated.

The Bush years ended with Stephen Harper in Ottawa having to consider the challenges of a new and very different administration in Washington. The border was as thick as ever.

Improving the Canadian game

The arrival in the White House of instinctively multilateralist President Obama should have promised a higher profile in Washington for traditionally multilateralist Canadians than it has thus far. Having lost the knack, we need to revive Canada's global value to deploy in Washington on vexed bilateral files. Perimeter security is such a strategic project. It shouldn't become politicized, though issues will certainly emerge in negotiation over the extent of information to be shared about residents of the two countries.

Showing the international community that Canada and the U.S. can successfully partner on Arctic issues will also send important signals. Circumpolar nations need, in the Arctic Council and elsewhere, to understand the consequences of the melting polar ice cap and assess and regulate navigational and mineral development opportunities, and also recognize the effects on Arctic settlements. There, the concept of a common North American perimeter can obtain meaning, not in the phony sense of Peter MacKay's imaginary threats from routine Russian military flights, but as a model and catalyst for sensible, forward-looking, cooperative stewardship.

North America is a solution zone, not a problem zone. It needs to include Mexico. The notion that the U.S. must deal symmetrically with its two borders is obviously misplaced, but Canadians mustn't let their possessiveness over Canada-U.S. issues block essential and beneficial three-way cooperation with Mexico wherever possible.

David Emerson has argued (in the February, 2011 issue of *Policy Options*) that the global competitive position of all three North American economies would benefit from more cooperation, especially with regard to energy and the environment. As "air, water, and ecosystems transcend national boundaries . . . the economics of energy and energy security ultimately demand North American solutions en route to global fixes."

Canada, at both the federal and the provincial levels, is far from coming up with creative thinking on climate change and other environmental files. Emerson warns that our "reputation and brand" can be easily destroyed by charges we are not dealing with carbon dioxide emissions and other related issues, including those at the North American level. Canada needs to remedy this neglect in order to garner positive political attention in Washington.

On the international peace and security files that top the list of Obama's preoccupations, such as nuclear proliferation, Canada must get back its edge. Canada should lead to enable the International Atomic Energy Agency (IAEA) to construct from the technical experience of the United Nations Monitoring, Verification and Inspection Commission (UNMOVIC) in Iraq a more secure and intrusive nuclear inspection regime. Verification issues in nuclear build-down are another long-standing Canadian vocation.

State-administered, anti-civilian chaos in Libya at the time of writing reminds us of Canada's leadership role in formulating the "responsibility to protect" doctrine a decade ago. Whatever the outcome in Libya, the U.S. would welcome the creation of a more effective international capacity for hard-power intervention legitimized by the United Nations Security Council. A 2000 Danish proposal for a Standby High-Readiness Brigade (SHIRBRIG) had to be shelved after several years of preparation because of inadequate international support. Canada, with its combat experience in Afghanistan, should take the lead to revive this essential idea.

On big transnational issues, Canada previously used our position in multilateral forums to punch above our weight. Today, we are absent even from key new international groupings such as the Trans-Pacific Partnership (TPP) initiative aimed at a multilateral FTA that includes Peru, Chile, and the U.S., but not Canada. The 2010 G-20 meeting in Toronto might have taken on cross-sectoral issues of importance and, among other things, created an enhanced profile for Canada in Washington. Of course, key issues couldn't be solved in Toronto, but the process might have been advanced usefully as happened on climate change between the fractious 2009 Copenhagen meeting and a more productive gathering in Cancun in 2010.

Conclusion

Canada needs an active and global foreign policy. As I once penned for Allan Gotlieb to in turn write for Trudeau to say, "We have important relationships in every part of the world."

Tackling international challenges has intrinsic merit for a country with an internationalist vocation. At the same time, the extent to which the U.S. is struggling economically and politically reinforces the case for more Canadian protagonism at the North American level.

The importance of Canada understanding the U.S., lifting its Washington profile, using social networks to connect to civil society, and supporting a North American research network (such as in the Canadian International Council's "GPS Project" report) cannot be overstated.

But success requires that Canadians again have useful things to say and to offer in North America and in the world. We need what Allan Gotlieb has stood for – the power of ideas.

Canadians can connect to Americans and the world in multiple ways in the interconnected and fragmented communications landscape we live in now. But ideas need to flow again from a vibrant public service, especially from the Department of Foreign Affairs, to be channelled by ambassadors (and their spouses) able to play in the major leagues as public entrepreneurs of ideas, in the way Allan Gotlieb has done, as an intellectually forceful deputy minister and ambassador. Elected government must again valorize such work. It is past time.

NEW FRIENDS IN THE DIGITAL AGE

David Malone

During a career that now spans over thirty-five years, many of them spent in the service of Canada's foreign policy in Ottawa and abroad, I have noted the strikingly consistent preference of many of my colleagues for transatlantic issues and relations. A smaller number preferred multilateral diplomacy, epitomized by postings in New York and Geneva, and a hardy minority, happily, was more attracted to the "global south" and its challenges. Countries in the latter group seemed to develop so slowly, Africa and Latin America becalmed by whole decades of stagnation, that the emergence of fast-growing large economies long eluded many foreign policy professionals, commentators, and academics. That the flavour of the times was no longer Brussels, but Beijing, came as a shock.

In Europe, seismic shifts in the rest of the world barely seemed to register. But Washington, always on the qui vive for developments that could enhance or undermine its commercial and geo-strategic interests, took early note of meaningful change in China, India, and, later, in Brazil and South Africa – change that in the former two was driven by economics, in the latter two by political change. Washington was sick of bickering with transatlantic allies (and sometimes those to the north), and was quite open to, indeed often excited about, the emergence of potential new partners that it sought to engage, both bilaterally and in new multilateral groupings.

For example, Washington, albeit at a great geographic remove, was always more open to a leading role for Turkey than were most of its allies. However, even Washington seemed surprised at the depth of change in Turkey over the past ten years, recognized by Barack Obama in 2009, during his first visit as president to a Muslim country. Its transformation from the "sick man of Europe" and fifth wheel of the Middle East to a rising power of unarguable relevance to several of the world's more acute crises (the Israeli-Arab conflict, the re-invention of Iraq, and Iran's quest for nuclear weapons) occurred while the West was at grips with internecine disagreements over Iraq. (Turkey had its own differences of perspective with both European and American approaches to its neighbour.) Early in the difficult engagement of NATO countries with Afghanistan, Turkey played an important and helpful role.

Quite recently, Washington and Brussels, each without measuring the possible implications of their stance, felt free to offend Turkish sensibilities: Washington in 2002–2003 as it prepared to invade Iraq, and Europe as it wrestled awkwardly with Turkey's candidacy for European Union membership. In other parts of the world, the significance of Turkey, obscured for many in the West by its erratic development track, its involvement in the Cyprus imbroglio, and its previously unimpressive politics, was always more clearly accepted, not least because in most of the world history is still thought to matter. Historically great nations like Turkey (and Iran), however controversial or objectionable their policies may be at times, are understood in the world at large to possess inherent international weight beyond whatever is convenient on any given day for the Western calculus.

———

In understanding the contemporary world, the prism of the digital age, teasingly proposed in this volume, with its enthusiasms both faddish and game changing, may not be overly helpful. Gigabytes of information can conceal more than they reveal, much of it disordered, inaccurate (sometimes deliberately so), and shallow. Tweets, digital columns, and the rest may entertain and briefly edify, but they don't do much to educate. And the countries of the West need a crash in-depth course on who is driving foreign policy in the rest of the world.

What is changing and what is not

A new international order emerges

During the 1960s and 1970s Japan and Germany stunned the world with their sharp economic recovery and political and social reinvention. But this simply served to reinforce the weight of the industrialized countries in world affairs. It was the rapid economic growth initiated in China by reforms after 1978, and in India after 1991, that were to undermine the cozy arrangements attending Western global domination. Their development profoundly upset the West's geo-political calculus and confounded Western commentariats. The European Union project recognized the benefits of a degree of consolidation in the West, but it has failed to sustain its momentum over the past decade.

In the Cold War era, the explicit project of Western hegemony and fantasies of *mission civilisatrice* through empire were abandoned. However, the enduring nature of Western domination (albeit challenged for a time by the Soviet Union) began to be seriously questioned only in the 1990s by some initially ignored Asian voices, including that of Singapore's Kishore Mahbubani (who was educated at Dalhousie University before rising to great heights in the service of Singapore).

But, of course, American military might and Washington's unique capacity for global reach often suggested imperial power, particularly after the Soviet Union's collapse in 1991. The unipolar moment, while brief, initially was taken to herald the lasting triumph of *Pax Americana*. In those early post–Cold War years, the steady if mostly low-key rise of China was still elusive to the West, much obsessed with the Balkans, the construction of the European Union, and the fight against terrorism that seriously taxed Washington's capacities and led to serious misjudgements.

American geo-strategists and defence analysts were more alert to changes in Asia than were most Western observers. But in the early 1990s, most of Washington would have been surprised by the emergence of China as a significant (if still economically immature) partner, and the U.S.'s only potential serious rival, by 2010.

As noted earlier, in South Africa and Brazil, politics held the key to change. The end of apartheid, a proud cross-party cause of Canada's in the 1970s and 1980s, signalled major changes in Africa as of the mid-1990s. It was South Africa's example, more than Western hectoring, that led to a greater focus on economic performance and improved governance in some countries. Today and in the foreseeable future, South Africa's economic interests in Africa are challenged more by China than by the Western powers that had for so long taken for granted their economic space on the resource-rich continent. And today joining China in building their profile and economic investment in Africa are India (whose trading communities have long dotted the African coastline) and Brazil, no longer confining its focus to fellow Portuguese-speaking African nations. Although presenting some risks, the rise of these new international actors is likely to benefit those African nations adopting an unsentimental view of all foreign suitors and a pragmatic approach to their blandishments. More competition to invest should be good for business on the continent, however much it seems to dismay many in the West.

Sixteen years of strong presidential leadership, first by Fernando Henrique Cardoso and then by Luiz Inacio Lula da Silva – each profoundly democratic but espousing different political and social preferences – was sufficient to set Brazil on a path of generally steady, unspectacular but compounding growth and of much greater self-confidence. The country became Latin America's giant in a way it had not been able to achieve in earlier post–World War II decades, having been governed for too long by inwardly oriented, self-serving civilian governments and by an inept military junta.

Although none of China, India, Brazil, or South Africa can hope to replicate the military clout or economic weight of the U.S. any time soon, with their emergence as meaningful partners for others, not only bilaterally, but also in multilateral forums from the World Trade Organization (wto) to the G-20, they have achieved a momentum that the West decisively lacks, particularly in the wake of the 2008–2009 economic and financial crisis.

Making new friends

The end of the Cold War provided an opportunity for governments the world over to reassess their foreign policies in order
to tailor them more closely to emerging realities. Few took
advantage of this opening. Tony Blair's "New Labour" in the
U.K. did adopt an often compelling advocacy on climate
change and the fight against poverty, but these essentially
optimistic themes were eventually drowned out by recriminations over the British role in the occupation of Iraq.

In the U.S., President George H.W. Bush's essentially
generous call for a New World Order in the wake of Iraq's
invasion of Kuwait soon foundered on the shoals of heightened partisanship in Washington and then on his son's mis-
conceived and financially ruinous ventures in Iraq and
Afghanistan.

In Canada, Foreign Minister Lloyd Axworthy developed a
creative "niche diplomacy" centred on the humanitarian
imperative and the fight against impunity. But the government sadly flubbed a chance to re-imagine international relations in a post–Cold War world during the Foreign Policy
Review of 1993–1995, implausibly promising to do more on
all fronts while initiating necessary if drastic budget cuts. Ten
years later, the Canadian government again attempted to
develop a grand schema for its foreign policy, and again it was
condemned to frustration and public indifference. On both
occasions, although both contemporary and foreseen global
changes were described with analytical rigour, Ottawa refused
to draw conclusions by making choices.

Meanwhile, most Western capitals had barely noticed
China and India engage in a quiet, but for them critical,

struggle, each intent on avoiding encirclement by the other (and its allies), nor Chinese efforts to loosen American dominance of sea lanes on the periphery of much of Asia. Also largely invisible to the West was India's re-engagement with Southeast Asia, in line with millennial patterns. With the exception of the U.S., Western countries did little to redouble their own engagement with Asia, while intra-Asian links and tensions intensified.

For Canada, well-meaning efforts to engage with emerging countries may have seemed to Asia too little, too late from a country some of them view as resource rich, sitting on enviable real estate, featuring very attractive pluralistic national and generous social models, but distinctly second-tier otherwise. Canada's success in warding off the worst of the 2008–2009 global economic and financial crisis, for which any number of national traits and politicians take credit, was noticed internationally, but did little to counteract Canada's loss of relative weight in international relations. A senior Brazilian visitor in mid-2011 witheringly described Canada as a "status quo" power, while another Brazilian perhaps more creatively described Canada as a "regional power without a region."

The case of India

India had long been considered the basket case of Asia, weighted down by hundreds of millions of hopelessly poor. Its foreign policy under Indira Gandhi had been petulant, displaying pronounced double standards even relative to those of the great powers. (To champion non-alignment while effectively allying with Moscow was not its only inconsistency.) India's nuclear test of 1974, seen by the U.S., Canada, Japan, and most others as a dangerous breach of the nuclear non-proliferation regime, accentuated the antipathy for New Delhi in the West. Further, India's decisive role in breaking up Pakistan in 1971 was viewed with great suspicion in most capitals, even though this saved millions of Bangladeshis from the ravages of the Pakistani army. In brief, as seen from the West, India was a pain.

Only area specialists understood that India's nuclear test was more than a gratuitous provocation – it represented an existential lunge for nuclear parity with China, after losing to Beijing a bitter border war in 1962. As to Indira Gandhi, she could be grating, but American policy towards South Asia was often confused: a sometimes toxic broth of good intentions, generous development, and humanitarian assistance, resentments over the mere notion of non-alignment, and Washington's tortured responses to local views on American challenges and failures in Vietnam. Delhi largely backed into its 1971 alliance with Moscow because of its worries over China (Pakistan's steadiest ally) and its perception that Washington was, at best, an unreliable friend.

Suivez Washington!

It was, of course, the U.S. that first noticed serious change in India as a result of economic reforms introduced in 1991 in response to a severe balance-of-payments crisis. Within years, the country was exhibiting strong economic growth. While the geo-strategic dimensions of American foreign policy tended then to attract more attention than Washington's international commercial drive (and still does), its determination, as of the late 1990s, to place the relationship with India on a new footing was driven perhaps most strongly by the emergence of a fast-growing market of over a billion consumers, however poor. The immediate impulsion, though, came from further Indian, and then Pakistani, nuclear tests in 1998 and a dangerous, if controlled, border war between the two countries in 1999. Although the clock ran out on the Clinton administration's efforts to secure a new range of understandings with New Delhi, the George W. Bush administration, during the years 2005–2008, succeeded in doing so.

Canada is simply trying to catch up, while Moscow salvages what it can of its defence relationship with New Delhi, and China contends with India as more of an equal (if one with an economy still less than a third the size of its own). Of the rest of the West, France and the U.K. have devoted the most sustained attention and are likely to reap the most sustained rewards.

Trade über alles?

Does a relationship with India based only on trade considerations make sense? At least it is a straightforward option, and Indians themselves are well practised in the promotion of their economic interests at the international level. But with India rather suddenly catapulted into the league of meaningful (if not yet fully "great") powers, is such a narrowly gauged approach sufficient? Indian notions of diplomacy involve much more, including cultural "soft power" and broader international relations elements.

With the exception of the U.S., U.K., and France, India's significant partners (including Canada) have focused on the economic and trade dimension of bilateral ties, with minor stylistic variations. But the short-term pay off of such efforts may disappoint. India today displays a deeper self-confidence than we have been used to, and it will accommodate the self-interest of others only to the extent that its own prevails above all. Thus, it may be wise also to develop other dimensions of the relationship (bearing, for example, on wider Asian issues and multilateral relations) and through them some additional leverage, as Washington, London, and Paris seek to do. For countries that today have less wind in their sails than India does, this can be difficult. India now matters more than they do, and Indian perspectives are entertained in major capitals much more than are those of even meaningful middle powers.

Status or stature – and for whom?

Given its unhappy colonial experience, and the wretched economic circumstances in which the country was left at the time of its independence, it is hardly surprising that India, a great nation throughout most of recorded history, should have proved very preoccupied with its place in the world and with building it up. This disposition is most evident today in the efforts of the Indian government to obtain a permanent seat in the UN Security Council. For India's external affairs ministry, how its partners react to this quest is not quite a litmus test, but close, as President Obama recognized by acquiescing to India's aspirations during his visit to India in November 2010.

India's leading partners in the West are prone to raise the question of whether India is prepared to assume global burdens (for example, in the fight against climate change), beyond its impressive contributions to UN peacekeeping, in exchange for greater recognition in the forums that matter. The "status quo" powers in the West tend to argue that a country should build up stature based on international performance before expecting much support for new institutional arrangements. But events have overtaken this debate.

Today, five to ten great and regional powers make the important decisions. India is increasingly a central actor within this group, for example as one of the five key negotiating actors in the WTO, likewise in UN negotiations on global climate change, and as a leading member of the G-20. It has not yet decided how much international burden sharing it is prepared to assume in order to justify such power sharing, but its policies of late suggest greater flexibility. Now that it plays in the big leagues, it will look to countries like Australia and Canada mostly in response to specific Indian economic and political requirements. For example, its need for uranium and its worries about Afghanistan represent issues on which India will be keen to engage both countries, even as it leaves them behind in term of global clout.

Challenges for Canadian diplomacy

The halcyon days when travelling Canadians were automatically meaningful visitors anywhere in the world are over. Our politicians and diplomats jostle for position in a crowded field in which the emerging countries benefit from momentum and others, well, don't. On the one hand, Canada is well known throughout much of the world, and mostly admired, sometimes liked. But that is no longer enough in a world on the move.

In order to engage the very busy emerging powers, Canadian international actors will need to offer not just varying degrees of economic access to our resources and markets, but also a wider sense that we are worth spending time with and on. Thus, Canadian diplomacy needs to develop comprehensive country and regional strategies that can induce emerging powers to engage with us. There is considerable evidence that thinking along these lines is well advanced in Ottawa, but at a time of serious resource constraints, it is not clear what Canadians are willing to give up domestically in the short run in order to matter more internationally and to prosper more as global actors in the medium and long term. And while there is much talk of a greater focus on diplomatic advocacy abroad, there is little effort to advocate within Canada for broader engagement with key new powers abroad. The government has acted to greatly increase the diplomatic assets targeted at China and India, and doubtless soon will do likewise with respect to Brazil, South Africa, Turkey, and Mexico. But a wider national engagement requiring greater political attention than minority parliaments tend to allow should now be possible after the May 2011 elections.

For example, might our universities and colleges serve as a platform for encouraging greater knowledge internationally of our assets and openness? And might they also serve as conduits of talented young Canadians towards emerging powers, on exchange or (if professors) on loan not with the intention of teaching something, but rather of learning a lot? If so, our constitutional arrangements and the inability of the provinces to agree on much joint action to promote the international profile and activities of these key national institutions provides little encouragement. Might the federal government provide greater inducement, perhaps focused on the research function of universities that it has played such an important role in upgrading over recent years? While federal funding is generally tight and likely to remain so for the next two to three years, a well-articulated strategy supported by the bulk of the provinces might well convince the government in Ottawa that this is a cause worth championing.

All governments are facing an urgent need, partly driven by the emergence of new technologies and social media, to update their diplomatic instruments. An exciting, Canadian-based project to develop a new *Oxford Handbook on Modern Diplomacy* suggests that virtually all serious students and practitioners of diplomacy see the diplomatic reporting function to be increasingly redundant (and sometimes counter-productive in the age of public access to even classified public information), with excellent analysis on country and regional developments available from such sources as the International Crisis Group and the Economist Intelligence Unit. Resources hitherto devoted to general reporting should clearly be redeployed to targeted information gathering and informed advocacy among key decision makers (and media commentators).

Canada's dilemma resembles that of others in the West, and, in terms of international identity and salience, it is less severe than that of several smaller players. The challenge arises from the fact that the West largely set the terms of the international game for the past three to four hundred years (challenged only by the Soviet Union from the late 1940s to the early 1990s). We are unsure of how we will fit in a new game in which Asia takes on greater weight and will need to share both burdens and responsibilities with the West. Tentative engagement through the G-20 has been modestly encouraging to date but clearly has not been assured or positive enough to guarantee active cooperation between key powers and regions in the future.

Models

One area in which Western countries, including Canada, will need to tread warily is in continuing to project their economic, political, and social systems as models for the rest of the world to follow. Western success long seemed worth emulating, but the emergence of India and China (each with a distinctive economic and political model hard to relate in their specifics to Western ones) challenges the notion that others are necessarily searching for Western solutions.

Developing countries need solutions that work locally, within the constraints of their existing reality and their history. The West's power of attraction, its "soft power," remains great; but, for example, early efforts to project Western approaches and models on Egypt's crisis of 2011 came a cropper, given the profound and age-old yearning of Egyptians for stability. And it is this important Egyptian trait that clashed with an immediate, urgent desire for change among frustrated cross-sections of Egyptian society to produce outcomes that, while positive, hardly conformed to Western ideals.

In brief, a model for Ecuador or Paraguay today might be Brazil – it certainly is not Denmark or Canada.

The contemporary influence of the media

At the time of writing, in 2011, the media are in flux. Print media are under tremendous financial pressure, with some proud publications, for example, the *New York Times* and its international edition, the *International Herald Tribune*, visibly wilting in scale and sometimes in quality. Other publications have, in relative terms, done much better, for example, *The Economist* (with booming sales figures at high prices), the *Financial Times*, and, in Canada, the *Globe and Mail*. Web-based media (to cite only American examples, *Slate*, *Politico*, the *Huffington Post*, and foreignpolicy.com) have often achieved very high levels of quality without yet proving that they can be profitable over time. Meanwhile, the web offers great freedom but often problematic quality in the absence of filters. Global actors are well aware of the opportunities and perils inherent in these shifts.

Websites (including print media ones) favour the sensational rather than the important – they want visitors to come back several times a day and keep having to reinvent the day's "news" to achieve this effect. Infotainment is catnip to the bored web surfer but the antithesis of serious news and analysis. By increasingly favouring the sensational, the media are arguably influencing international relations none for the better, insofar as governments spend a great deal of time reacting to a glut of both media stories and media non-stories, as well as the related commentary, that they fear could cost them politically. Communications teams are expanding, often in the absence of anything much to communicate (beyond obviously self-serving press releases, instantly discounted by the media).

The outcome of tectonic shifts in the global media is hard to foresee. Will subscribers be willing to pay more to achieve better value, added through high-cost writing and editing? Some examples suggest that there is indeed an audience out there for exactly this type of expensive globally oriented coverage. On the other hand, will those brought up to consider that everything on the web should be free be prepared to pay for quality news and analysis? We don't yet know. And, to a degree, the nature and quality of future diplomacy depends somewhat thereon.

Social media

As these lines are written, the globe is mesmerized by television images of Tahrir Square in Cairo, where opponents and supporters of President Mubarak have been jostling with each other to an uneasy standoff, with the Egyptian army pondering its next move. Much has been made of the role of social media in Egypt and in the uprising, weeks earlier, in Tunisia, that forced a seemingly unshakable dictator from office.

Social media can and do facilitate mobilization. But revolutions have been organized quite effectively for centuries without social media. In 1978–79, the Iranian Revolution was influenced by radio broadcasts of Ayatollah Khomeini and other regime opponents from points abroad. But it spread, as such revolts generally do, through local human communication by any available means. Likewise, the June 1963 anti-regime riots in Iran, fomented by conservative clerical interests, occurred in spite of the absence even of telephones for most of those involved. The last significant uprising in Egypt, the so-called bread riots of January 1977, mobilized larger numbers than the contemporary upheaval has to date in Cairo, through only word of mouth and limited access to foreign radio. Indeed, while the Mubarak regime reacted to the early evidence of mass unrest by shutting down the Internet and most phone service (as well as certain Arab broadcasts it thought particularly damaging), it wound up restoring these functions only days later, with the unrest apparently uninfluenced one way or the other.

Did people rise up in Cairo and Alexandria because of the availability of social media or because an ossified, self-serving regime had stayed in power too long, exhausted its welcome, and exasperated large numbers of educated but jobless or underemployed young people? Certainly the media, including social media, transmitted throughout the Arab world the depth of Tunisian frustration with the Ben Ali regime, and this served as a spark for events in Egypt and, subsequently, in Bahrain, Yemen, and Syria. But it is worth remembering that the rolling Arab revolutions of the 1950s occurred with the benefit of only "old media" communications.

Economic and political fundamentals drive events, including shifts in global power distribution. Methods of communication do not, although those challenging the established order of course adapt their strategies to whatever available instruments may best serve their purpose. A sense of history, of how today's protest movements, revolutions, and conflicts relate to those of previous generations, might be more useful than media enthusiasm over the role played by social media. The latter are at best facilitators, but certainly not drivers, of events such as those in Egypt.

How, in the heat of the moment, to interpret the WikiLeaks dump of thousands of U.S. diplomatic communications in

2010 and 2011? Will they alter international relations? Many of the leaked documents embarrassed Washington (occasionally Ottawa also) and irritated those mentioned in the dispatches. But it seems unlikely that this epiphenomenon will undermine the need of governments to engage each other, often confidentially (at least for a time). Very few "revelations" contained in the messages surprised knowledgeable readers; the more cynical among them may have been struck by the extent to which confidential U.S. diplomatic messages by and large conformed with U.S. public positions. American diplomats came off, in general, as more lucid than might have widely been supposed among their critics. That said, American diplomatic reporting on the corruption and foibles of rulers in Egypt and particularly in Tunisia were often cited by those driving the uprisings in those countries to support their actions.

Just as conversation (and its close cousin, gossip) is the lifeblood of most enduring human relationships, so are their diplomatic equivalents with regard to the intercourse of states (and between their servants). Will we be more cautious for a time? Undoubtedly. But Julian Assange seems more likely to be remembered as the Ned Kelly of the digital age than as a decisive figure of the twenty-first century. Certainly, in India, where everything the government says or does leaks, generally very quickly, the WikiLeaks cables were less of an inconvenience to the government than were contemporary leaked tapes of cell-phone conversations between a lobbyist and the great and the good of the country. And while Indians were agog over some WikiLeaks revelations, mostly the leaks addressed yesterday's news in every sense.

None of this is to make light of a highly relevant trend in global affairs today: the trivialization of much news, the triumphant emergence of infotainment, and the growing marginalization of serious analysis of world events in the pages and on the websites of a very small number of media organizations. Somewhat counteracting this trend is the reality that, so far, cost-free web availability of much of the high-quality analysis has been accessible by billions of individuals around the world. But there is not much evidence that it is widely preferred to more mundane offerings on the web.

Envoi

One challenge in international relations is not so much to recalibrate all activity in light of the emergence of social media, but rather to figure out how to make effective use of such media in responding to more fundamental shifts.

The emergence of the more multipolar world so many had called for over the past twenty years may well prove positive for the fight against poverty, the adaptation to and mitigation of climate change, the defeat of key infectious diseases, and in many other ways. But it is unsettling, as well as exciting. For us in the West, to be displaced from the dominant, if not exclusive, leading role in decision making is a new experience. This new situation confronts us with our ignorance of much of the world, and our past unkindness and injustices towards it. Rather than requiring others to adapt to our models, we will need to adjust to and respect some of theirs.

Young Canadians appear intrigued by the challenge, although not always necessarily possessing the tools to make a success of the engagement. For those of us who are older, changing our ways of thinking, our frames of reference, is much harder. But change we must.

Technological breakthroughs may help us, but they will only serve to accelerate change. Globally minded Canadians are better equipped than most to succeed in such a world, economically, diplomatically, and otherwise. Our own economic and social successes, the core of Canada's "soft power," serve us well in engaging the world. But we need more knowledge in order to connect effectively.

Allan Gotlieb will not be surprised by the central role the U.S. plays in this essay, although he might well, doubtless rightly, contest the related analysis. Madeleine Albright's breathtakingly self-confident assertion that "we stand tall and we see further than other countries into the future," continues, it seems, to have currency. While Washington's engagement with emerging powers has been uneven and undermined by occasional setbacks, the U.S. has been determined and optimistic on this score. The rest of us follow and might perhaps do so more enthusiastically.

part three
foreign affairs at the centre

WHERE IS HEADQUARTERS?:
Diplomacy, Development, and Defence

Elissa Golberg and Michael Kaduck

Afghanistan, Haiti, Sudan, Guatemala.
All of these are considered "fragile" or "crisis-affected" states, and represent some of the messiest and most challenging contexts in which Canadian federal departments and agencies are involved. When you survey the landscape of foreign policy today, fragile or crisis-affected countries are most vulnerable to internal and external shocks, and least likely to meet the Millennium Development Goals. They suffer from a nasty combination of political violence, organized crime, corruption, and poverty, and their governments are often unwilling or unable to meet the needs of their citizens.

The dynamics of such countries spill over borders and often call for international action because they represent a threat to regional or international security, including for Canada. Fragile states require of us a special kind of patience, modesty, and humility. They also call on us to pursue new kinds of cross-departmental cooperation, and to be innovative with our tools and partnerships in highly insecure environments. They demand that diplomacy, development, and defence engage with each other in ways they have not often done before – not just to work in proximity, but to collaborate in pursuit of a unified objective to advance Canadian interests.

And all this must be done amid the reliably hyperbolic 24/7

media glare of the digital age and an increasingly planetary attention deficit syndrome. The impetus to do something, or at least to be perceived as doing something, is combined with a fear of unlimited liability, of quagmire. This stimulates wildly unrealistic expectations about reconstruction, stability, and effective governance in countries that may have taken decades to reach their present malaise.

Clearly Canada and other governments and organizations working to meet the challenges presented by fragile states face significant challenges. How can we make the best use of the assets that we have to get positive results? These assets – including aid, investment, diplomacy, police, and soldiers – come from different departments and agencies. How can we work through the differences across department cultures and processes so that the best from each can work together on the ground without debilitating bureaucracy, rivalries, and turf wars? How can diplomats, generals, and development specialists coordinate in real time so that we can enable an integrated team on the ground that is nimble and effective?

We have used many different organizing concepts in recent years to describe the kind of collaboration that is needed to work in such complex places. We have talked about "3D," or Diplomacy, Defence, and Development; "3C," or Coherent, Coordinated, and Complementary; as well as "comprehensive," "whole-of-government," and "whole-of-system" approaches.[1] Ultimately, the aim has been to underscore that no one department or agency (or even country) has all the tools on its own to achieve positive results in fragile and crisis-affected states. We will need multidimensional efforts, and we will need to incorporate a range of civilian and military expertise. Pre-globalization constructs that fostered silos and sectoral distinctiveness have been Blackberried, tweeted, and Facebooked into oblivion.

We need to encourage the development of shared analysis and integrated strategies from the outset, and work hard to foster a better appreciation of one another's corporate cultures. Effective responses to crises are both swift and subtle. Bringing together diplomacy, development, and defence, actors can multiply either the positive or the negative dimensions of our organizational distinctiveness, depending on how our teams are socialized and led. Therefore, we need to enhance our flexibility to deal with the Rumsfeldian "unknown unknowns" without so synthesizing our policies across government that our approach becomes a Seinfeldian "show about nothing." The objective is not to make the unique characteristics of military, police, diplomatic, and other civilian practitioners disappear, but rather to create an environment in which each can bring his or her own knowledge and talents to bear to craft a more effective Canadian effort that makes the best use of the resources that we have.

We are not looking for homogenization. Rather, the distinct strengths brought by the security "boots" on the ground, along with the "shoes" of politics and governance and the "sandals" of social and economic development are all required. The practical application of 3D does not mean Canadian departments or agencies become like one another; it does not even require that they like one another. Instead, it demands that they work constructively together to create effects consistent with shared government objectives and with a wider set of partners in the international system, including the private sector and NGOs. What we are ultimately trying to describe is much less a policy or a set of discrete behaviours than a state of mind founded on true partnerships. In this sense, the diplomacy of the twenty-first century requires cultural change among departments of our government at home as well as abroad.

Can 3D really work?

It is hard to achieve this kind of change in attitude and approach. Really hard. It demands that departments and agencies think, plan, and act comprehensively and collaborate from the outset. It has important financial and human resource implications. It calls for compromise and a willingness to dilute one department's agenda to promote the efforts of another to arrive at a better outcome. This can raise serious and uncomfortable questions about who leads, who follows, and when. Generally, senior officials have no appetite for this debate; the issue gets resolved in practice, as diplomacy, development, or defence pulls into the lead depending on the context. At the end of the day, for integrated whole-of-government efforts to work, officials have to want to make these adjustments and sacrifices, and it needs to be reinforced and rewarded by their organizations as well as by politicians and civil society.

Canada has demonstrated that it can adapt, as illustrated by the painful evolution of our engagement in Afghanistan. The government was able eventually to establish a joint vision, and use its diplomatic, development, and defence capabilities to achieve results in an extraordinarily complex and challenging environment.

Afghanistan has been a difficult learning experience for the

Canadian government. Both military and civilian officials had to figure out how to operate in a complex counterinsurgency in the context of a larger NATO-led operation. For the first few years of Canada's presence in the country, key departments and agencies concerned with the engagement operated largely independently of one another, with only rudimentary cooperation.[2] Information was shared, but only partially, and activities were not coordinated. There was no unified set of objectives or results.

When we look back at the period of 2005 to 2007 in particular, we can see how departments and agencies, in the absence of clear policy objectives and systems of governance, failed to collaborate effectively to achieve lasting effects, despite the expenditure of considerable blood and treasure. The military was focused almost exclusively on the subnational level in Kandahar, while the Canadian International Development Agency (CIDA) and the Department of Foreign Affairs and International Trade (DFAIT) continued to give priority to investments at the national level with more modest projects based out of the Provincial Reconstruction Team (PRT). In Kandahar, the military established tactical and operational plans that were not tied to governance or development objectives or capacities. This, combined with insufficient troops, made an effective "clear and hold" strategy virtually impossible. Soldiers fought again and again to retake territory they had taken only months before. At the same time, there were too few civilians present, frustrating their military counterparts. The handful of Foreign Affairs political officers, Canadian civilian police, and CIDA development officers had a difficult time prioritizing activities and keeping up with and feeding into the military who vastly outnumbered them, and who often treated their civilian counterparts as guests and not as partners.[3] Consequently the military often assumed a lead role on policy or program matters because they had the resources to reinforce their vision. The other departments ceded by default.

WHAT DOES 3D MEAN FOR DIPLOMATS?

The diplomatic dimension of the 3Ds is critical because, in essence, all our efforts in fragile states come down to shaping the international environment on behalf of Canadians. Diplomacy reflects who we are, how we want to be perceived, and what we want things to be like – all at the same time.

If we agree that diplomacy is not peripheral to our effectiveness in fragile states, and that DFAIT will need to be an active leader and participant in 3D efforts, then we need to change some important policies and practices. We need to modify the way diplomacy is funded, how staff are trained, and how the foreign ministry is organized. We need to provide the department with redundant staffing capacity to swiftly deploy people who are pre-trained to work alongside military personnel, with knowledge of conflict contexts, and with appropriate support structures. We will also need to allow people to move around, within, and outside the foreign ministry so it can tap into necessary knowledge, capacities, skills, and field experience.

At one illustrative meeting during this period, senior military and civilian staff came together for a meeting at Kandahar Airfield to discuss progress made in a village that had been "cleared" of insurgents by Canadian Forces operations a few months earlier. At the time, it had been agreed that the military would stay and create an enabling context for governance and development. The civilians had committed to reach out to Afghan and international partners to initiate stabilization activities. In the intervening period however, the military, believing the insurgents had left the area, had determined it needed to redirect its very limited forces to another area of the province. The civilians, who had spent considerable energy working to identify projects and convince NGOs and Afghan government officials to work in the area, felt abandoned, as their partners were now under threat by insurgents who had returned to the area once there was no longer a military presence. The meeting was tense – frustrations mounted and recriminations flew from both sides. The military pointed to statistics, including of the diminished numbers of "troops in contact," and insisted the area was safe for development to begin. They highlighted polls in which Afghans in the area said they wanted access to basic services. The civilians had their own evidence and maps showing where partners would not work for fear of being attacked after having received infamous threatening "night letters" from the Taliban. There was no mutual appreciation of what was required to make progress in the area.

It was a powerful lesson in the need for shared expectations, joint planning, and execution. Ultimately, even though they lived and worked in the same province, the military and civilian staff did not possess the same analysis or have the same interlocutors, and were not working towards the same objectives to enable the government of Afghanistan to extend its reach and influence in Kandahar. Things were equally disjointed in headquarters, and by 2007 civilian-military relationships had become, on some files, downright hostile. These difficulties were starkly highlighted by the "Manley Panel," which called for a wholesale change in Canadian strategy.[4]

With the space created by the panel, several critical changes were implemented. A senior civilian representative, the "RoCK" (Representative of Canada in Kandahar), was deployed to oversee all civilian efforts; to act as a counterpart to the Canadian Forces Task Force Commander and ensure civilian-military cohesion; and to be the main civilian interlocutor with Afghans and international NGOs at the provincial level. In Ottawa and in the field, a new whole-of-government strategy was developed. Canadian government approved six overarching priorities that reflected Afghan and international concerns, as well as three signature projects to capture Afghan imagination. Metrics were developed to help communicate with both Canadians and Afghans about intended achievements, and to determine whether the plan was on track.

AMBASSADORS OF WHAT?

One recurring obstacle to the smooth functioning of multidisciplinary operations is the lack of shared views on the role of the Canadian Head of Mission (HOM) in a country where operations are taking place. In some cases, especially when there is a sudden, large Canadian Forces presence in a country, the HOM can be perceived by officials – in Ottawa and in the field – not as the ambassador of Canada, but as the ambassador of DFAIT. Not only is this wrong and unhelpful, but it is also hard to overcome, and there have been many differences of opinion regarding Heads of Mission and military task force commanders as to exactly who is advising whom. The distinction between chain

> of command and civilian authority is real and important, but military rank should not be seen as overriding the formal and legitimate role of the ambassador.
>
> The ambassador is uniquely placed, qualified, and authorized to bring together the many threads of Canadian interest and responsibility, and to ensure greater coherence in what Canada is trying to do.

These priorities tied the Canadian Forces, DFAIT, CIDA, and other government partners together in a framework of mutual accountability that had hitherto not existed. A Canadian civilian "surge" saw the number of deployed diplomatic, development, correctional, and police personnel rise from fifteen to sixty-three between May and August 2008.[5] At Kandahar Airfield, the Provincial Reconstruction Team, Forward Operating Bases, and Canadian civilian and military staffs were co-located to encourage a shared assessment and to enable joint action drawing on one another's contribution.[6] New civilian program tools were also created to allow for greater agility and flexibility at the local level, and delegated authorities were provided to match those accorded to the military.[7] A civilian heading our development projects, for example, now had the authority to commit funds without checking back with headquarters in Ottawa. A synchronization board was established at the PRT to coordinate project-level implementation.

Additionally, a unified civilian-military plan for the province, initially referred to as the "Kandahar Action Plan," was developed (the first of its kind), and tactical and operational plans were increasingly tied to governance and development objectives, with civilian and military counterparts designing these plans together and synchronizing their activities to enable tangible counter-insurgency results.[8] For instance, civilians from the PRT began to live in the districts as stabilization officers and collaborated with their military colleagues to bring Afghan government and PRT program resources to places like Zhari and Panjwayi in ways never done before, as a direct result of a shared civilian-military assessment and strategy. The quality of Canada's effort was greatly enhanced, and became a model for other nations, including the United States.

These changes were evident, for instance, in how Task Force Kandahar approached the aftermath of the June 2008 Sarposa Prison break.[9] A test for the nascent civilian-military joined-up approach, civilian and military officials quickly developed and implemented an integrated strategy. Military engineers and security experts supported civilian diplomatic, corrections, and police staff as they developed plans to address the deficiencies in perimeter security at the facility that were presented to the Afghan Ministry of Justice. The RoCK drew on delegated funding to initiate emergency reconstruction activities which were completed within a week, with contracts and specifics developed by the Canadian Forces. Support for affected local business was initiated by CIDA. The response by Canada to what had been a devastating insurgent strategic communications success was quick, targeted, and effective, restoring confidence among the Kandaharis.

These improvements in field-level cooperation did not occur in a vacuum and were achieved in part because the necessary resources and authorities were put in place at headquarters. In early 2008 an Afghanistan Task Force (ATF) was established at the Privy Council Office, mandating an integrated approach and common narrative among departments, and empowered to direct and enforce that mandate. The task force brought much-needed discipline to diplomatic, development, and defence efforts, and contributed to the transformation of Canada's involvement in Afghanistan from a counter-insurgency campaign with no clear objectives to a joined-up campaign aimed at achieving a limited number of objectives by a specific date. The ATF acted as the secretariat for the Cabinet committee that provided much-needed sustained political direction and oversight. Together, these two enabled additional civilian staff to be deployed, and mandated the delegated authorities and autonomy to the representative of Canada in Kandahar, a critical element in a quick, nimble response to local developments. Establishing new structures and processes, including joint exercises and training and the creation of communities of practice between the field and headquarters around the six priorities, resulted in enhanced collective effort. Departments began to learn one another's language and culture, and joint strategic planning became much easier.[10]

The resources and political will behind our Afghanistan effort were without parallel in Canada during the post–Cold War era. Direct engagement by the prime minister, Cabinet, Parliament, and the clerk of the Privy Council prompted the necessary push to a more integrated effort and a coordinated use of Canadian assets on the ground. Serious foreign policy endeavours require serious leadership and serious commitment of effort.

Working together, the Department of National Defence, DFAIT, and CIDA have shown that a comprehensive and successful effort is possible on other major files. The catastrophic earthquake in Haiti in January 2010, which killed some three-hundred-thousand people and displaced a further 1.5 million, is a recent example. The disaster was met with timely and determined collaboration among Canadian diplomacy, development, and defence, working well together in real time. No undertaking on this scale is possible without some fog and friction, but overwhelmingly the government's response was fast, appropriate, and made a difference in the lives of Haitians (and Canadians) in distress.

This success did not arise by chance but from sustained and deliberate effort across government departments. Little-known but vital systems of cooperation and collaboration, joint training, and liaison officers helped each organization develop an appreciation of what others bring to the table.

Over the course of a decade, an interdepartmental structure has evolved, led by DFAIT,to guide government responses to natural disasters abroad.[11] It now includes a set of standard operating procedures that have been tested and are regularly refined through whole-of-government after-action reviews, a standing interdepartmental natural-disaster task force that is available around the clock, a rapidly deployable assessment capacity that is cross-departmental in character, and a set of tools that have been developed to play to Canadian strengths and to meet urgent needs consistent with international principles.[12] While not without its hiccups, this standing capacity enabled a swift and effective Canadian response to the earthquake. Lessons from Afghanistan were adapted for Haiti. The deployment of Foreign Affairs stabilization and CIDA humanitarian officers, co-located with their Canadian Forces colleagues in Jacmel and Leogane, enabled joint analysis of the local context and joint decision making, and similar liaison officers were exchanged in Ottawa. Joint decision making, aided by the task force and senior-level coordination mechanisms, produced a single set of objectives which could then be executed.

Can it all be replicated and where do we go from here?

Our experience in policy, programming, and operations for fragile states like Afghanistan and Haiti tells us the benefits of 3D are worth the effort and risks. And risks there are, to be sure. It is human nature to revert back to what is comfortable, and "comfortable," for government officials, means working vertically within our own organizations. Pursuing a more joined-up approach rarely fits tidily into news cycles or even fiscal years, but it makes what Canada does internationally more effective than if we approached it as individual departments and agencies.

The tricky, hazardous, marvellous thing about aligning our diplomacy, development, and defence activities is that the effort itself causes us to question our own assumptions and accustomed practices. If public servants or politicians choose to advance or celebrate those who serve silos over those who embrace the space that connects them, then we will safely and comfortably substitute activities for achievements. This, sadly, is what many expect – that we will do the minimum and call it a masterpiece. But this does not advance Canadian interests.

It is absurd to expect officials to enable a "comprehensive approach" on an operation as though they were changing a toner cartridge or a magazine. We need to practise this kind of coherence constantly if it is going to work in Ottawa and in crisis zones. If we really want to maximize our diplomatic, defence, and development investments, we need organizations and managers to stop rewarding parochialism and start acknowledging, explicitly and materially, success in cross-departmental coordination.

Interagency collaboration can be improved. Personnel exchanges, joint training and planning, effective "lessons learned" exercises, standard operating procedures, and interoperable communications platforms can each make a meaningful contribution, as can joint accountability in performance metrics. Whole-of-government working groups in specialized areas like security system reform can help build a shared approach, or at least a common awareness of aims and means. Personal commitment and leadership at the most senior levels of the civilian agencies and the Canadian Forces to continue to building a true interagency partnership will go a long way to transforming the success of what Canada does abroad.

Encouraging multilaterals like the UN and NATO to get their own act together is another, longer story, but that is something Canadian departments and agencies can constructively work on together (and the subject of another essay).

All of this is possible; none of it is magic.

We need to advocate for each other's success in the commander's tent and at the budget table, with smart investments not just in defence but also in civilian departments and capabilities. To do less than this is to do less than Canadians deserve of us all.

Notes

1   See www.3c-conference2009.ch.

2   Canada's presence can be divided into essentially three periods: 2001–
    2005 (with the re-establishment of an embassy in Kabul and the
    deployment of the Canadian Forces to Kabul as part of the UN opera-
    tion); 2005–2008 (the deployment of the Canadian Forces to Kandahar,
    and Canadian responsibility for the Provincial Reconstruction Team);
    and 2008–2011 (post–Manley report, significant civilian "surge," joint
    civilian-military collaboration, and transfer to the Americans the
    responsibility of Kandahar Province).

3   Even computer systems were incompatible, with civilian and military
    personnel using different classified and unclassified systems, making
    it difficult even to share reports and analyses. The playing field was
    also uneven between the military and civilians. The Canadian Forces,
    by virtue of organizational culture, training, experience, and spending
    authorities, is better designed for expeditionary missions such as
    Afghanistan. The civilians needed to build this capacity from scratch,
    creating systems to identify, train, and sustain people in the field, and
    to support families at home, while delivering results alongside the
    Canadian Forces in a hyperchallenging environment.

4   There were positive developments, beginning in 2007, with the crea-
    tion of the coordinator position at DFAIT for Afghanistan at the asso-
    ciate deputy level and the re-organization of DFAIT's Afghanistan Task
    Force, the increased role of the Head of Mission in Kabul, and the
    deployment of an initial senior civilian in Kandahar. (From
    Independent Panel on Canada's Future Role in Afghanistan, the
    Minister of Public Works and Government Services, January 2008,
    http://dsp-psd.pwgsc.gc.ca/collection_2008/dfait-maeci/FR5–20–1-
    2008E.pdf.)

5   The number of civilian federal public servants working in Kandahar

as of February 2011 is seventy-seven, with another forty-one working in Kabul.

6   This co-location at the district level was further advanced with subsequent rotations of military and civilian staffs, and Canadian district stabilization plans.

7   The RoCK was provided with up to two million dollars in signing authorities for CIDA and DFAIT projects through the Global Peace and Security Fund and the CIDA Kandahar Local Initiatives Program.

8   It is worth noting here that people do matter. There was strong collaboration and mutual trust among the military command team of Task Force Kandahar and the RoCK, which facilitated considerable change.

9   On the evening of June 13, 2008, an insurgent raid on the Sarposa prison in Kandahar resulted in the escape of some 1,100 prisoners. The Government of Canada disbursed people and funds rapidly as part of an eventual commitment of up to four million dollars for reconstruction and ongoing programming at Sarposa.

10   While this essay cannot address all aspects of the mission, it is worth highlighting the disappointing lack of attention that was paid by the media to the civilian effort, particularly in Kandahar.

11   This structure is led by the Stabilization and Reconstruction Task Force housed in Foreign Affairs. START was established in 2005 with a mandate to enhance whole-of-government collaboration and capacity to respond to fragile and crisis-affected states.

12   The toolkit includes, among other things, cash contributions in response to appeals, deployment of relief supplies maintained by CIDA, deployment of Canadian experts both from within and outside government, or the use of Canadian Forces assets. Other special measures may also be used in exceptional circumstances such as debt relief, immigration fee waivers, or a matching fund mechanism.

A CANADIAN DEPARTMENT OF GLOBAL AFFAIRS?

Kim Richard Nossal

One of the major paradoxes of diplomacy in the digital age is that the expanding nature of what constitutes "foreign policy" makes it increasingly difficult for governments to organize themselves coherently and effectively to engage in global politics. The expansion of foreign policy has been accelerated by the globalization of the economy, the growth in both number and scope of transnational actors, and the mounting complexity of international operations. But governments continue to organize themselves in ways that reflect an earlier age. Virtually all governments in the contemporary international system maintain separate bureaucracies to engage in a wide range of activities beyond their state's borders: foreign ministries to conduct general political relations with other governments; ministries to encourage foreign trade, sometimes twinned with the foreign ministry; agencies to collect intelligence and conduct espionage operations abroad; agencies to engage in financial coordination with other governments; agencies to monitor and control the country's borders; departments to deliver development assistance abroad; and armed forces to act in military or policing operations beyond the state's borders. This way of organizing the state reflects organizational decisions taken long ago, but these have often persisted for largely inertial reasons. And in this panoply of bureaucratic organizations, the foreign ministry has a particularly problematic role, since there are so few agreed-upon parameters for what should be within its purview. Indeed, foreign ministries, with their traditions and practices deeply rooted in European history, seem old-fashioned and out of touch, unsure of their mission in an increasingly networked and globalized world.

Reflecting on the problem in the British context, Peter Hain, minister of state in the Foreign and Commonwealth Office, noted in 2001 that the concept of the "foreign" in foreign policy was becoming harder and harder to define. He entitled his reflection *The End of Foreign Policy?* and wondered whether there would eventually come a time when "international policy" would "no longer be split into arbitrary compartments," and foreign ministries would be rebranded as departments of global affairs.[1]

Some parts of Hain's suggestions would be more easily accomplished than others. For example, it is relatively easy to embrace the change in language from "foreign policy" to "international policy." Paul Martin, Canada's prime minister from December 2003 to February 2006, chose to use "international policy" to describe all those areas of policy that are part of the Canadian government's engagement with the international system. His government's *International Policy Statement*, published in 2005, consisted of reviews of diplomacy, development assistance, defence, and international trade, with an overview presented by the prime minister himself.[2]

But it is much more difficult to embrace the other part of Hain's argument to create an appropriate bureaucratic structure for "international policy." How exactly is this to be done?

A number of governments in the late 1990s and early 2000s adopted a variant of what the Labour government of Tony Blair had first bruited in 1997 as "joined-up government" – a recognition that there are some intractable social problems that cannot be solved by a single government agency alone, but which require the integrated and coordinated efforts of different agencies. Blair's joined-up government morphed into what was called a "whole-of-government" approach to policy, according to which different agencies would work to provide integrated policy formulation and implementation that crossed department lines.[3] A complementary approach was embraced in the case of international stabilization missions: the so-called 3D approach to foreign policy, which sought to integrate the contributions of the defence forces, the development assistance agencies, and the diplomats from the foreign offices.

But whole-of-government and 3D approaches, in particular as they were applied in international stabilization missions in the former Yugoslavia, in Afghanistan, and in Haiti, demonstrated the difficulties of overcoming "departmentalism" in policy terms. The whole-of-government approach sought to integrate the operations of a number of different departments, each with different organizational missions, different bureaucratic cultures, and different bits of bureaucratic turf to defend. As long as the structures of hierarchical authority are left in place, with each department funded separately, each responsible for its particular mission, each reporting separately to a central authority, the essential unity of purpose implied by the whole-of-government rhetoric simply will not work.

Peter Hain's proposal for a singular Department of Global Affairs was intended to address the fragmentary dynamics of departmentalism. In this model, the bureaucracy would be radically reorganized so that the "arbitrary compartments" of policy areas would be brought into a single ministry charged with the formation and implementation of "international policy." Instead of multiple semi-autonomous organizations, with their own hierarchical structures, with their own institutional cultures, and with their own champions at the political level in Cabinet vying for budgets and control over policy "turf," there would be one Department of Global Affairs, with a single internal hierarchical authority, represented by a single voice at the Cabinet table. Such a departmental structure would logically bring all the "compartments" together under one roof. In other words, all those who formulate and implement a country's engagement with the world would be members of this mega-department: the diplomats, the members of the armed forces, the spies, the development assistance specialists, the immigration and border-control officials, and all the functional policy experts from the "international" units of "domestic" departments.

On the one hand, there can be little doubt that entrenched departmentalism can be challenged and indeed overcome through bureaucratic reorganization. The most extensive government reorganization in the contemporary era – the creation of the Department of Homeland Security (DHS) in the United States in the aftermath of the attacks of September 11, 2001 – demonstrates what can be achieved when one takes twenty-two different government agencies, many with long histories and deeply rooted organizational traditions and cultures, and hurriedly repacks them into a single organization. The case of DHS suggests that one can indeed remould institutional cultures and create a singular organizational mission.

But the DHS case also begs an obvious question about large-scale government reorganization: even if the creation of a single Department of Global Affairs would provide the state with an effective bureaucratic organization for the formulation and delivery of "international policy," would the massive reorganization necessary to effect that change be worth it?

The Canadian experience with foreign policy reorganization suggests one answer. In Canada, effort to grapple with the role of the foreign ministry in a world where the definition of foreign policy is changing goes back more than a generation. While the issue was first raised in the early 1970s with the creation of the Interdepartmental Committee on External Relations, it was not until Allan Gotlieb was appointed as the deputy minister of the Department of External Affairs (DEA) – or the under-secretary of state for External Affairs, as the position was known then – that efforts were made to address the problem in a sustained and structural way. Gotlieb's idea, in the late 1970s, was to reposition the Department of External Affairs within the Ottawa bureaucracy and give it a central role in the making of international policy. In Gotlieb's view, External Affairs should become a central agency, like other central agencies of the Canadian state, such as the Privy Council Office, the Prime Minister's Office, the Treasury Board Secretariat, and the Department of Finance. And, like other central agencies in Ottawa, External Affairs should be given authority to engage in a broad coordinating role across government, advising Cabinet as a whole on a range of foreign policy issues, rather than running programs.

This movement included the consolidation of the Foreign Service, bringing together those civil servants from External Affairs, International Trade and Commerce, Immigration, and other government departments who served abroad. Introduced in 1980, the consolidation also saw all the senior officials serving abroad in the Department of External Affairs, the Department of Industry, Trade and Commerce (IT&C, as it had become in 1969) and of Employment and Immigration (E&I) integrated into External Affairs. From this common pool were drawn the heads of posts for Canada's missions around the world. The idea behind this scheme was to allow posts abroad to operate more efficiently by streamlining the authority of the head. Instead of having to coordinate the activities of officials at a mission abroad who were receiving instructions from External Affairs, the Canadian International Development Agency (CIDA), IT&C, and E&I in Ottawa, the head of post would have authority over all staff, regardless of their function.

The final component was the reorganization of the government by Prime Minister Pierre Elliott Trudeau on January 12, 1982. All departments with an economic mandate were affected. A new central agency, the Ministry of State for Economic and Regional Development, replaced the Ministry of State for Economic Development; the Department of Regional Economic Expansion and the "industry" side of the Department of Industry, Trade and Commerce were both replaced by a Department of Regional Industrial Expansion. The "trade" side of IT&C, including those parts of the Trade Commissioner Service not included in consolidation, as well as the Export Development Corporation and the Canadian Commercial Corporation, were all merged into a "new" Department of External Affairs.

However, the 1982 reorganization did not resolve any of the bureaucratic "turf" issues that continued to appear as other departments continued to pursue their international policy mandates. The attempts of External Affairs to establish its primacy over all aspects of international policy produced mixed results, and DEA lost control of the most important foreign policy area: the negotiation of a free trade agreement with the United States. The Progressive Conservative government of Brian Mulroney decided to create a separate agency to guide the process of negotiating that agreement. Usually, international negotiations on trade would be conducted by External Affairs, but Mulroney's Cabinet decided that this issue was too important to be left to one department; rather it would be given to a Trade Negotiations Office (TNO) under a chief negotiator, Simon Reisman, and staffed by officials seconded from other agencies of government like Regional Industrial Expansion, Finance, External Affairs, and the Privy Council Office (PCO), with some drawn from outside the bureaucracy. While Reisman was nominally a deputy in External Affairs and the TNO was nominally an administrative unit of that department, in fact the TNO was an autonomous organization that reported directly to the prime minister.

The tinkering with the foreign ministry continued in the late 1980s. The name was changed in 1989 to External Affairs and International Trade Canada (EATIC), and when Reid Morden was appointed under-secretary of state for external affairs in the early 1990s, there was yet another change in direction. Under Morden, the department went "back to basics" – focusing only on political and economic affairs and eliminating overlap. This required transferring some roles to other departments. External's immigration function was moved to Employment and Immigration Canada; responsibility for international expositions was moved to Communications

Canada; international sports was transferred to Fitness and Amateur Sport; cultural and academic programs were moved to the Canada Council (a measure that was subsequently defeated in the Senate).

In one policy area, however, EATIC continued to try to extend its policy control. The reorganization in 1982 had left the Canadian International Development Agency alone, and during the 1980s Joe Clark, as the minister responsible for both External Affairs and CIDA, had allowed CIDA considerable policy autonomy. After Mulroney moved Clark from External Affairs to become the constitutional affairs minister in 1991, however, the Cabinet decided to put funding for both official development assistance (ODA) and assistance to the former Soviet Union and Eastern Europe into one budget envelope. The International Assistance Envelope (IAE) was controlled by External Affairs, which sought to shift large amounts of development assistance funds to spending on projects designed to assist Central and Eastern European countries in making the transition to democracy.

After the Liberals under Jean Chrétien came to power in November 1993, the Department of Foreign Affairs and International Trade (DFAIT), as it was renamed by Chrétien, experienced a serious shrinkage in size over the course of the 1990s as part of deficit reduction. By 2001, the size of the department had been reduced to 1,900 Foreign Service officers, 2,800 non-rotational officers in Canada, and 4,600 locally engaged personnel in foreign missions. The problem for DFAIT was that policy demands did not diminish with the shrinking resources. Because the number of independent countries grew in the wake of the Cold War, there were always good reasons to expand the number of diplomatic posts maintained by Canada, and so while some embassies abroad closed, many more were opened. The activities of the Canadian government in international organizations increased as new organizations like the International Criminal Court were created, and negotiations in the institutions of global governance increased and became more complex. The number of Canadians travelling abroad during this period expanded as well, requiring expanded consular services.

The pressures on DFAIT accelerated in the post–9/11 period, when a new emphasis was placed on the 3D approach in initiatives such as the Canadian mission to Afghanistan. DFAIT increasingly worked with CIDA and the Department of National Defence (DND) to coordinate activities abroad, particularly in Canada's expanding commitment in Afghanistan. However, this increasing focus on the integration of the activities of the three departments abroad was interrupted by Paul Martin's decision to pull DFAIT apart. On December 12, 2003, the day that he became prime minister, Martin announced that the Department of Foreign Affairs and International Trade would be divided into two separate departments again, bringing to an end twenty-one years of fusion. He made this announcement without any prior discussion or consultation with affected industry groups such as the Canadian Manufacturers and Exporters.

Although the Martin government used an Order-in-Council to split the department, the legislation to give the two new departments their new formal mandates was never passed. By the time that legislation was ready to be considered by Parliament, the 2004 election had reduced the Liberals to a minority government, and on second reading, the three opposition parties in the House of Commons combined to defeat this government bill – the first time since 1925 that a government bill was defeated on second reading.

When the Conservative Party of Canada under Stephen Harper won a minority in the January 2006 elections, the bureaucratic landscape did not change much. One of its first acts on taking office was to cancel Martin's Order-in-Council; Harper also confirmed the continuing responsibility of the Department of Foreign Affairs and International Trade for the coordination of the international policy agenda. In the past five years, however, more power and authority over Canada's international policy has accumulated in the Prime Minister's Office and the Privy Council Office.

In short, in the thirty-three years since Allan Gotlieb first proposed the idea of External Affairs as a central agency in 1977, no amount of fiddling with the foreign policy bureaucracy has managed to resolve the essential dilemmas that Gotlieb and his contemporaries were trying to address. While today the Department of Foreign Affairs and International Trade continues to have the formal central role for the coordination of foreign policy that it enjoyed for much of the twentieth century, the bureaucratic landscape remains as crowded as ever with those agencies responsible for key elements of Canada's foreign policy: at the centre, the clerk of the Privy Council, the foreign and defence policy adviser to the prime minister, located in the Privy Council Office; the Department of National Defence and the Canadian Armed Forces; CIDA; the Department of Finance, Treasury Board Secretariat; and Public Safety Canada, with its various agencies that are involved in national security, including the Canada Border Services Agency, the

Royal Canadian Mounted Police, and the Canadian Security Intelligence Service.

It is precisely this profusion of bureaucratic actors "delivering" international policy on behalf of Canada that may make the idea of a Department of Global Affairs for Canada seem attractive. A single agency, with a single deputy minister and a single voice in Cabinet, responsible for *all* aspects of Canada's international policies – widely defined – would indeed introduce an element of coherence and coordination that is difficult to achieve when the power over policy formulation is tightly centralized at the centre – in the Prime Minister's Office and the Privy Council Office – and at the same time policy implementation is fragmented across a number of bureaucratic actors.

The irony, however, is that while a Department of Global Affairs might be *conceptually* attractive, actually trying to put into place a bureaucratic structure that takes seriously a whole-of-government approach in international policy would be an administrative – and hence political – nightmare for any government in Ottawa that sought to bring such a mega-department into being.

First, there is the simple and highly pragmatic consideration that reorganizing the bureaucracy comes at an exceedingly high price. Thus, for example, when the Harper government took office in February 2006, they were determined that, as one Conservative put it, they "would not get involved in a complicated rejigging of the machinery of government . . . basically for the reason that if you start to reorganize the machinery of government, you kiss your productivity goodbye for two years as everyone figures out who reports to whom."[4]

Second, absent the kind of transformative event such as 9/11, which allowed the administration of George W. Bush to trump the entrenched interests of twenty-two government agencies and create a single Department of Homeland Security, no government in Ottawa could even attempt to tidy up the foreign policy bureaucracy without generating backlashes at several different levels.

Consider, for example, the insurmountable difficulty of trying to fit the Canadian Armed Forces into this scheme. To be sure, at a purely conceptual level, there is no logical reason why the legislated four-fold mandate of the CAF – protecting Canada, defending Canadian sovereignty, defending North America, and contributing to international peace and security around the world – could not be delivered in a different way. The CAF command structure could be left intact, with the chief of defence staff responsible to the minister of global affairs rather than the minister of national defence. The Department of National Defence could be abolished and incorporated as a unit of the Department of Global Affairs, whose deputy minister would have responsibility for policy and resources. But what might seem conceptually tidy would simply be unthinkable from a realistic political perspective. What government – unless motivated by a rare death wish – would actually move to abolish the Department of National Defence and put the armed forces of the country into an agency filled with diplomats, tradies, intelligence agents, development assistance experts, immigration officers, customs and border agents, and a variety of other officials whose policy areas have global implications?

Importantly, it is likely that the very same dynamic that would make the dismantling of DND and the transfer of the

CAF to Global Affairs politically impossible would be reproduced in other policy areas. The resistance to dismantling a large number of established federal institutions – DFAIT, CIDA, CSIS, CBSA, and all the international units of other government departments – would be considerable. The effects on the smooth functioning of the Canadian state would be profound (since the world would not stop while Canada reorganized itself). And the process of putting a new bureaucratic Humpty back together into a single coherent organization would be fraught with practical difficulties.

In short, it is the high costs and the "unthinkability" of bureaucratic alternatives that gives the present structures their inertial fixedness rather than any inherent logic in the way in which governments are organized. But a look at the alternatives – and what happened in Canada when significant attention was devoted to trying to rejig the machinery of government to make it more coherent and tidy – strongly suggests that it makes considerable sense simply to leave Hain's "arbitrary compartments" alone, and just live with the inherent messiness that comes with how governments organize themselves for foreign policy.

Notes

1   Peter Hain, *The End of Foreign Policy: Britain's Interests, Global Linkages and Natural Limits* (London: Fabian Society, 2001), 61.

2   *Canada's International Policy Statement: A Role of Pride and Influence in the World.* (Ottawa: Department of Foreign Affairs, 2005).

3   Tom Christensen and Per Lægreid, "The Whole-of-Government Approach to Public Sector Reform," *Public Administration Review* 67, no. 6 (2007): 1059–66.

4   Quoted in Paul Wells, *Right Side Up: The Fall of Paul Martin and the Rise of Stephen Harper's New Conservatism* (Toronto: McClelland & Stewart, 2006), 283.

REMAKING THE DEPARTMENT OF FOREIGN AFFAIRS AND INTERNATIONAL TRADE

Drew Fagan

A few days before Christmas 2008, the Department of Foreign Affairs and International Trade (DFAIT) launched a year-long series of conferences and other public events to shine a little light on itself in its centennial year.

An open house was held at the department's distinctive ziggurat headquarters in Ottawa. A commemorative stamp was issued by Canada Post. A multi-panel display was produced to highlight Canadian diplomats' role through the decades (carefully balancing, in pictures and text, the role of Liberal and Conservative ministers).

The opening event was a conference on the singular individuals of departmental lore, from Vincent Massey and Hume Wrong to Sylvia Ostry and Allan Gotlieb. But it was fitting that on the Department's one-hundredth anniversary the capstone conference event – the annual O.D. Skelton Memorial Lecture – would be about Oscar Douglas Skelton himself.

"As under-secretary of state for external affairs from 1925 to 1941, he transformed the Department of External Affairs from a bureaucratic backwater into Canada's pre-eminent institution of government, recruiting officers of the first rank, marshalling systematic policy advice, and laying the groundwork for a diplomatic service," said Carleton University professor Norman Hillmer.[1]

Although left unacknowledged, it was impossible that evening not to compare the circumstances of yesterday with today. Who today would describe DFAIT as "Canada's pre-eminent institution of government"? And what could be done to bring back some of DFAIT's lost influence?

The later conferences focused more on the department's future. Indeed, the location of the conferences – Vancouver, Calgary, Saskatoon, and Montreal – marked a departure for DFAIT, and was an attempt to reach out to the international affairs community. As it ramped up hiring to replace retiring baby boomers, departmental officials hoped the conferences would spark greater interest from academics, analysts, and students interested in a career in diplomacy.

Within weeks, however, recruitment would be pared back. By the actual anniversary of the department's founding on June 1, 1909, DFAIT's two-billion-dollar-plus budget was under severe strain.

For years, DFAIT had cried poor while recording surpluses. For years, Liberal and Conservative governments had complained about the handling of DFAIT resources and had constrained DFAIT's budget. And now, as press articles focused on embassies cutting travel and entertainment expenses, there was little sympathy in Ottawa – it was more like schadenfreude.[2]

The simple truth is that DFAIT is the department Ottawa loves to hate. DFAIT officials look forward to spending up to half of their career living in global capitals, while the rest of the bureaucracy makes do in Canada's quiet, cold capital city. Canada's diplomats are seen as generalists in a specialist's world, as spendthrifts in a time of thrift, as anachronistic in an information age.

And that's just among fellow bureaucrats. Among politicians, the assessment is even harsher.[3]

One lengthy article assessing Prime Minister Stephen Harper's government took special aim at DFAIT. Canada's embassies are viewed, the article stated, as a problem to be managed, not an asset to be utilized. One Cabinet minister described the diplomatic corps as a "self-satisfied coven of right-thinking high priests."[4]

Equally telling was an adjoining reference to how the Harper government and the bureaucracy often work well together despite spasms of mutual suspicion. The U.S. requirement that Canadians carry passports had threatened to overwhelm the passport system and MPs' complaint lines. Canada's passport offices are run by a special agency under DFAIT, and the backlog was eliminated in "double-time," leaving the Conservatives impressed. And yet, there was no reference in the article to this being a DFAIT success in a critical area: service delivery to the growing number of Canadians who work, travel, and live outside the country.[5]

It is a perfect example of a phenomenon that DFAIT officials remark upon: policy failures are pinned on DFAIT while policy successes are government successes stripped of their DFAIT input. But that is what happens when one's credibility is near low ebb.[6]

It's not as if DFAIT has been blind to how it is viewed and what it must do. While deputy minister of foreign affairs from 2003 to 2007, Peter Harder said DFAIT encapsulated what former dean of MIT Lester Thurow describes as "the challenge of incremental decline." The government – and Harder's point didn't alter as leadership changed from Jean Chrétien to Paul Martin to Stephen Harper – "[does] not always see us in an indulgent light," he said. Instead they see "bricks and mortar in the shape of residences and embassies." They ask: "What do we get for all this money?"

Behind the scenes, the department is responding. DFAIT is building capacity on a narrower range of priorities and avoiding the replication of work done in departments with international branches of their own, as well as recalibrating its mission network. Though public attention has focused on a handful of mission closures, DFAIT has opened more missions in key emerging economies, especially China and India, but also in Mexico, Brazil, and the Persian Gulf. After a bobbled start, DFAIT is expanding its staff in key existing missions, synchronizing this with reducing a bloated staff in Ottawa. And DFAIT is adding resources to its trade and consular services, including construction of a state-of-the-art Emergency Watch and Response Centre in Ottawa to oversee the government's reaction to international crises.[7]

"We have to be realistic and acknowledge that international relations in a globalized world affect everybody," said Foreign Affairs Deputy Minister Morris Rosenberg. "The department can't just talk to itself."[8]

DFAIT is hardly alone in facing these challenges. Every foreign affairs ministry is grappling with what amount to existential questions: How can they be more effective in an age of instantaneous communication? How can they maintain their role when nongovernmental actors may matter more than government? Can they be a "central agency" within government when virtually all departments are international – from the core players of defence, aid, and immigration, to others such as Health Canada, which must engage internationally on pandemics? And can they adapt to the age of summitry when government leaders increasingly meet face to face?

In 2006, Michael Jay, who was then retiring from the top position at the Foreign and Commonwealth Office in London, said, in terms familiar to Canadian diplomats, that the FCO was viewed in the Prime Minister's Office as tending "to see both sides of a question when seeing one is quite enough." Jay noted that even Queen Victoria had thought the invention of the telegraph would mean "the time for ambassadors and their pretensions is past."[9]

Clearly, Queen Victoria had something in common with Allan Gotlieb. The need for foreign ministries to adapt to globalization and the communications revolution is commonly viewed as being of recent vintage. But Gotlieb, like Queen Victoria, saw it coming. Indeed, he began his tenure in 1977 as under-secretary of state for External Affairs (the position now of deputy minister) with clear views on what to do. Until Gotlieb, most deputy heads of the department had spent their entire career there. But after spending barely a decade at External Affairs, as it was then called, Gotlieb spent nine years as deputy minister of Communications and deputy minister of Manpower and Immigration before taking over the corner office back at the Pearson building.[10]

During his tenure, Gotlieb found that Communications had a substantial international branch. Manpower and Immigration – this during the nascence of multiculturalism when Canada began to cast its net more widely for immigrants – also didn't much bother to check in with the foreign ministry.

When Gotlieb returned to External Affairs, he did so with chips in his pocket from then–Prime Minister Pierre Trudeau, though Trudeau was no fan of the diplomatic corps. The department needed the capacity to coordinate foreign policy, at a minimum to be *primus inter pares*. In other words, Gotlieb wanted the department to be a central agency within the government, and he made much progress. The government integrated into External Affairs officials serving abroad in other key departments. The goal was to consolidate in the hands of each ambassador greater authority over the mission.[11]

"I fought like a tiger for that."[12]

But as Gotlieb himself admitted in a 1979 speech, there are different types of central agencies. The Treasury Board, which oversees departments' expenditures, is one kind. Departments can't avoid Treasury Board. External Affairs, even after consolidating its international network, was another kind because it had no sanctioning power, Gotlieb noted, and had to rely "largely on informal arrangements."[13]

If anything, the situation is more challenging today. Here too, Gotlieb was prescient in understanding why. He entered the department in 1957, at the height of what he described in a 2004 speech as "High Pearsonianism," and when the department was known as among the best in the world, but not in all things. The best minds focused on multilateral diplomacy and the protection of the Western alliance. But what of more prosaic issues such as consular services or Canada-U.S. border problems? These elicited little interest: "The magnetic pull of Canada's international vocation was overwhelming; the bread-and-butter issues had no pull at all," Gotlieb said.[14]

The Department of Communications might have set up its own international branch regardless of the attention paid to its issues at External Affairs. So might most of the two dozen departments and agencies that now have staff posted at

Canada's missions. But External Affairs contributed to this profusion of international operations by failing to do enough to look after the country's everyday interests. The department needed to be a behemoth that kept pace with the growing range of international issues, or it needed to become the acknowledged leader of a network that brought together the disparate levers of international policy.

Instead, it remained a department too much like the others – in bureaucratic language, "imbued with verticality in terms of its corporate design and culture."[15] It stood apart, and others stepped into the breach.

There remains a pecking order at DFAIT to this day that reflects this history. The international trade side of DFAIT – though often better managed, relatively better resourced and certainly better focused – is still commonly viewed as less prestigious. DFAIT operations – such as budget and human resources, and the care and feeding of Canada's network of 173 missions – is receiving greater attention, but still is seen by some as a box to be checked off. And within the foreign affairs side of the department, which accounts for the majority of DFAIT's budget, responsibility for security and multilateral files have pride of place over bilateral issues with individual countries.

In any case, DFAIT may only now be emerging from more than two decades of challenging circumstances. The Department of National Defence characterized the 1990s as its "lost decade," when scandal and budget cuts tarnished its image and capacity, but DND has made up lost ground in recent years. Its budget began to grow towards the end of the Chrétien era, accelerated under Paul Martin, and has met with particular favour under Stephen Harper. DFAIT's nadir was reached between 2003 and 2006 – when Paul Martin split the Department and Stephen Harper put it back together.[16] But DFAIT is still struggling, and its budget – while not much more than one-tenth of DND's – is still under pressure from cutbacks.[17]

The heart of an international affairs ministry is international. This sounds self-evident, but for years international affairs ministries haven't operated that way. They have increased the size of headquarters, but failed to maintain adequate resources at missions. The main reason is budgetary: it costs more to keep a Foreign Service officer abroad. But failure to maintain resources is also rationalized on the basis that the Internet has eliminated the tyranny of distance.

No country took this to heart like Canada. DFAIT headquarters is a rabbit warren, housing far more staff than it was designed to handle. During the 1990s era of deficit elimination, the mission network was cut and has never recovered. Today, DFAIT is easily the most headquarters-heavy ministry in the G-8.[18]

DFAIT's leadership knows this imbalance is its greatest hindrance. "We are not alone in thinking that the tools and approaches we've relied on for generations may not be the most efficacious," Len Edwards, then–deputy foreign affairs minister, told staff in 2008. "Other countries are thinking the same. The United Kingdom, the United States, Australia, France, and others."

Simply put, DFAIT can be successful only if Canada's network of embassies, consulates, and trade offices is effective under DFAIT leadership. This is DFAIT's central agency role: to be the guiding hand (and landlord) for Canada's eyes and ears abroad.

What does this mean? It means being more strategic in how one operates.

Empower the ambassadors

Before Arif Lalani was named Canada's ambassador to Afghanistan in 2007, he sat down with no fewer than five deputy minister–level officials (the clerk of the Privy Council, the prime minister's national security adviser, Defence, the Canadian International Development Agency, and DFAIT). As a result, Lalani could hold himself out as someone who represented much more than DFAIT, which proved to be invaluable in Kabul. Still, there were limits to the principle of ambassador as true head-of-mission. The United States and Great Britain had made more progress in eliminating stovepipes. "They were living the principle and we were still trying to establish it," Lalani said.[19]

Ambassadors often leave on posting with little buy-in from other departments. They don't even necessarily go with a clear set of objectives. It's not often necessary to get the support of multiple deputy ministers, but "mandate letters" signed by key departments is de rigueur in other countries. Without this, ambassadors can hardly be what they should be: the closest thing an international affairs ministry has to a general.

Empower diplomats' public engagement

In a world of ubiquitous information, Canadian diplomats are almost silent. They risk censure if they speak publicly without approval from Ottawa. The outcome is that Canadian diplomacy is often one step, or two, behind the news cycle. While the U.S. State Department makes use of Twitter to respond to events or deny Internet rumours, Canadian government communications are highly centralized, ensuring the often tardy release of information.

The effect of this information counter-revolution is broad and deep. DFAIT's public diplomacy budgets have been slashed. Even before the reductions, Canada spent less than other Western countries. Likewise, DFAIT has cut back on Internet strategies to engage with students and other informed observers on topical issues.

Allan Gotlieb is credited with perfecting the art of broader diplomatic engagement, including public diplomacy, while he was ambassador to the United States. The Canadian embassy became a destination for cultural events and Canadian diplomats moved beyond the State Department to focus on a wider array of players – Congress particularly, but also state governments, think tanks, lobbyists, and other influencers. The further afield one goes from the safe confines of diplomat-to-diplomat discussion, the greater the opportunity for engagement, but also the greater the chance for complication and embarrassment. Today there is, necessarily, little appetite for risk at DFAIT.

Such reticence is also evident in the degree of public information available about what DFAIT does.[20] All Canadian departments produce an annual planning report, but they are written in a fashion best understood by bureaucrats. By comparison, the Foreign Office in London has published a concise and readable business plan for the next five years with timelines for important milestones.

Empower diplomats' policy making and reporting

The policy process at DFAIT is skewed. Policy emanates from Ottawa to mission, with inadequate input from those posted abroad. It is a reflection of the days when information flows were time consuming.

But progress is being made, in line with other foreign ministries. DFAIT is experimenting with communications techniques to allow staff at headquarters and mission to work together on policy initiatives in real time. Furthermore, the initiative to move staff abroad includes experiments in policy priorities. A DFAIT centre on Arctic policy is being established in Oslo, as is a centre on Latin America policy in Bogotá.

Integral to the policy process, as well, is strong reporting from missions. Too often, though, departmental reports replicate information available on the Internet. (This remains a common affliction among foreign ministries.) There is also inadequate coordination among missions on issues of broad interest and inadequate recognition that coordinated reporting might be of value beyond DFAIT, including with carefully selected nongovernmental partners. The common rationale for not distributing reports beyond government is that they contain sensitive information. But the vast majority of the thousands of diplomatic cables leaked by WikiLeaks were hardly sensitive. Many reports could be distributed more broadly if ministries were more realistic in assessing what is truly highly sensitive information.

Empower the accountants

Canada's missions cost DFAIT more than one-third of its budget. But it wasn't until three years ago that DFAIT established a full internal operation to ensure that all the players in the mission network – DFAIT, other federal departments and agencies, and three provinces (Ontario, Quebec, and Alberta) – were well looked after. The department now has better growth estimates, which is critical when dozens of missions operate at full capacity. It also is reducing costs by centralizing back-office functions. (The new centre for Europe, the Middle East, and Africa is located in an industrial park near Heathrow airport.)[21]

But other foreign ministries are moving faster. Denmark has outsourced mission operations, for example, while Great Britain is accelerating the sale of surplus properties, including some official residences. DFAIT is not unlike many foreign ministries: property rich and cash poor. But despite much analysis, DFAIT has been able to sell few holdings or, for that matter, to keep up with repair and rehabilitation of properties.[22]

Build partnerships and open up processes

Unlike the foreign affairs side of DFAIT, the international trade side has a clear mandate: to increase Canadian trade and investment. Its global commerce strategy has accelerated the signing of free trade and foreign investment and protection agreements. Most new missions have been trade-focused, and the department has invested in Internet technologies to better connect Canadian companies with departmental trade and investment information.

Simply put, the international trade side of DFAIT often seems better suited to twenty-first-century diplomacy. It has been more aggressive in profiling its services at home and driving expansion of DFAIT's seventeen domestic offices. It is building closer partnerships with the private sector to refine sector strategies, including by creating trade commissioner positions in national industry associations. It views itself, in sum, as building a network of players – Canadian multinationals, small and medium-sized businesses, industry associations, trans-national corporations – to drive Canada's prosperity.

The foreign affairs side of DFAIT is not as far advanced. Secondments from other departments are uncommon, from outside government even more so.[23] It could do more to reach out systematically to the expatriate Canadian community. Canadian multinationals often are better placed than diplomats to analyze events (they're dealing daily with local regulations) but engagement tends to be fitful on the foreign affairs side. The same tends to be true for NGOs.

DFAIT is a smaller player every year in terms of Canada's overall international role, as nongovernmental participants become more influential. It needs to continue to adapt, just as other foreign affairs ministries are struggling to do, and situate itself as a coordinator of a growing band of those working to strengthen the Canadian interest and project Canadian values globally.[24]

The department's younger officers recognize this. They might as easily have joined an international company or an NGO as DFAIT (and probably do expect to spend part of their career working in such organizations).

They also know better than anyone that the stereotypes of their profession are false. Canadian diplomats are more likely to be posted to one of dozens of hardship missions than to be living on the Seine. They are more likely to be riding in an armoured vehicle than in one that is chauffeur-driven. They are more likely to be learning Mandarin than, say, Italian. And DFAIT still only hires 1 per cent of job applicants. For all its challenges, DFAIT is still a sought-after employer. The next Allan Gotlieb may be working there now.

Notes

1 Conference presentations were collected in Greg Donaghy and Kim Richard Nossal, eds., *Architects and Innovators: Building the Department of Foreign Affairs and International Trade, 1909–2009* (Montreal and Kingston: McGill-Queen's University Press, 2009).

2 Campbell Clark, "Mission Improbable: Diplomacy on the Cheap," *Globe and Mail*, November 13, 2009.

3 I took an unusual route into DFAIT. I was appointed by the non-partisan Public Service Commission. I had been Ottawa bureau chief for the *Globe and Mail*. Upon learning of my career change, I was told, then–Prime Minister Paul Martin remarked that I'd be "just like the rest" at DFAIT within a year. He didn't mean it as a compliment.

4 Paul Wells and John Geddes, "What You Don't Know about Stephen Harper," *Maclean's* 124 no. 4 (February 2011): 14.

5 Ibid.

6 Amid the usual criticism, former Prime Minister Brian Mulroney said governments should take "full advantage of the brilliance and the innovation" of DFAIT. His international initiatives, Mulroney said, had DFAIT's imprimatur, including the Canada-U.S. free trade agreement. However, DFAIT had a secondary role in those negotiations. Since then, DFAIT's role in Canada-U.S. relations has been similarly circumscribed. See Jennifer Campbell, "Mulroney Champions 'Brilliance' in Foreign Service," *Ottawa Citizen*, February 17, 2010.

7 Department of Foreign Affairs and International Trade, *Report on Plans and Priorities 2010–11* (Ottawa: Foreign Affairs and International Trade Canada, 2010), 5.

8 Fen Hampson, "Total Diplomacy: A Conversation with Morris Rosenberg," *Diplomat* 21 no. 4 (Fall 2010): 13.

9 Michael Jay, "Foreign Policy and the Diplomat: The End of the Affair?" (Speech at the London School of Economics, London, July

27, 2006). Jay added that he had once asked then–Prime Minister Margaret Thatcher how she squared her hostility to the Foreign Office as an institution with her admiration for those Foreign Office officials with whom she had worked. "Oh, that's perfectly clear," she said. "I trained them myself."

10 The three most recent deputy ministers of foreign affairs – Morris Rosenberg, Len Edwards, and Peter Harder – were all previously deputies of other departments. So too was Louis Lévesque, the deputy minister of international trade.

11 Michael Pitfield, who was then retiring as clerk of the Privy Council, explained in 1982 that he expanded the department's role in spite of itself. The department perpetuated "a guild mentality" and "could not run itself very well," Pitfield said to Foreign Service officers, adding it had been given "a chance to show itself worthy or be cast into irrelevance."

12 Allan Gotlieb, in conversation with the author, February 2011.

13 Allan Gotlieb, "Canadian Diplomacy in the 1980s." (Speech presented at the University of Toronto's Centre for International Studies, Toronto, February 15, 1979).

14 Allan Gotlieb, "Romanticism and Realism in Canada's Foreign Policy." (C.D. Howe Institute Benefactors Lecture, Toronto, Novermber 3, 2004).

15 Andrew Cooper, "Vertical Limits: A Foreign Ministry of the Future," *Journal of Canadian Studies* 35 no. 4 (Winter 2001): 111.

16 The division of DFAIT still rankles. It also proved problematic in, of all places, Seoul. South Korea had modelled the merger of its foreign affairs and international trade departments on Ottawa's 1982 amalgamation. Korea's foreign minister was troubled enough to seek an explanation for the split from the Canadian embassy. The minister, Ban Ki-moon, is now secretary-general of the United Nations.

17 In 2007, DFAIT volunteered to be among the first departments to take

part in a budget reallocation exercise. DFAIT proposed to boost the mission network. The plan to add four hundred staff abroad and cut headquarters by four hundred – on a staff complement of ten-thousand-plus – is only now moving forward because inadequate controls meant headquarters growth continued.

18   DND and CIDA also are headquarters-heavy and have embarked on strategies to put more staff in the field. "Quite frankly, we have to take folks from headquarters and put them back in field units," Lt.-Gen. Andrew Leslie said. See Carl Meyer, "Too Many Senior Officers in Ottawa Desk Jobs," *Embassy* (March 2, 2011): 1

19   Arif Lalani, in discussion with the author, February 2011. A review by the U.S. State Department emphasized that ambassadors need a better understanding of all agencies in their embassies. Chiefs of Mission, wrote Secretary of State Hillary Rodham Clinton, must have "the tools [to be] ... the Chief Executive Officer of a multi-agency mission." See Department of State, *Leading Through Civilian Power: The First Quadrennial Diplomacy and Development Review* (Washington D.C.: Department of State, 2010).

20   In 2007, DFAIT streamlined its priorities, focusing on Afghanistan, North America, and the Western hemisphere, and emerging markets, especially China and India. DFAIT has also worked to build capacity in the key areas of peace and security, trade and investment, international law, and human rights. See Alan Freeman, "Top Bureaucrats Take Aim at Ottawa's Diplomats," *Globe and Mail*, June 29, 2007.

21   Overall staffing strategy at Canada's 173 missions now rests with the DFAIT-chaired Deputy Ministers Committee on Representation Abroad. This structure now is to be used to better coordinate policy initiatives too.

22   DFAIT's sale of the ambassador's residence in Dublin in 2008 was controversial, though its isolated location (near the home of U2 singer Bono) made it problematic. DFAIT's underutilized properties include

what may be its most valuable: the Canadian high commission in Grosvenor Square and Canada House in Trafalgar Square.

23 Is a professional Foreign Service fundamental or might recruitment of outside talent revitalize higher-level ranks? See Eugene Lang and Eric Morse, "Why There's No Canadian Holbrooke," *Ottawa Citizen*, December 28, 2010, and Paul Heinbecker, "Diplomacy Is Not a Job for Amateurs," *Ottawa Citizen*, January 6, 2011.

24 There is no end of examples of foreign ministries adapting. The Netherlands has moved away from fixed posting terms, leaving experts in the field longer to build deep alliances. It also has agreements with Dutch multinationals to hire "trailing" spouses of Foreign Service officers. New U.S. Foreign Service officers are expected to do a posting in a hardship mission before moving to one in the developed world. The Foreign Office in London is opening the process for filling senior positions, including placing recruitment notices in *The Economist*.

THE NATIONAL INTEREST

Edward Greenspon

Canada went to war in Afghanistan in the autumn of 2001. Ten years later, our soldiers continued to participate in a low-grade but persistent conflict that has cost the treasury billions of dollars and military families the lives and limbs of their loved ones.

Was the national interest served by all this commitment to a military venture that lasted longer than the First and Second World Wars combined? It would be difficult to judge since Canadians participated in very little discussion about where the national interest lies and whether the fate of Afghanistan rates as a vital interest.

We first dispatched troops as part of the posse going after Osama bin Laden. Did we do so because twenty-four Canadians were killed in the World Trade Center? Or was it simply part and parcel of our solidarity with the United States, our commitment to NATO, or the cover provided by the United Nations? Or all three? Did it later become a politically palatable means of pacifying the Bush administration for our noisy non-intervention in Iraq or our bumbling rejection of Ballistic Missile Defence? How influential was hawkish Rick Hillier's preference for Afghanistan over Darfur? Was the mission motivated by an analysis that it was better to kill scumbags on their soil before they could besmirch ours? And why did we persist in the face of illiberal and corrupt Afghan behaviour to support a supposedly evolving democracy, to stabilize a failing state, to make it safe for girls to go to school, to build a massive dam? Or was it a result of nothing grander than policy inertia?

All these explanations were trotted out at one time or another. Without a clear articulation of the national interest, Canada subjects itself to a fog of policy confusion and weakens the fibre of democratic accountability. If our Afghan commitment is justifiable, it needs, in any democracy let alone a digital-age democracy, to be justified. "We are in Afghanistan because we are in Afghanistan" is not a good enough answer. The clear articulation of the national interest provides an anchor for policy makers beyond the politically expedient.

When I travelled around the country in 2009 and 2010 as chair of a Canadian International Council panel, experts attending our sessions often counselled that the greatest contribution we could make would be an unequivocal recitation of Canada's national interests. Asked afterwards for their own such description, many of our guests tended to, well, equivocate.

It seems that when it comes to national interests, exhortations are often preferred to the hard labour of exploration and explanation. It's worse than the weather: it seems everyone wants to talk about it, but few are prepared to state anything useful.

In some ways, you can't blame people. Identifying national interests is an exercise that either tends toward the trite (security and prosperity, anyone?) or leads into a labyrinth as complex as the nation itself – take the worldviews of founding nations, founding peoples, distinct societies, vertical mosaics, diverse communities, provincial fiefdoms, etc., etc., and then project them onto the global stage. The head spins. Moreover, defining broad interests creates ready targets for the partisans of narrow interests. It is certainly safest for practitioners to keep their heads down and proceed à la carte and to define the national interest post hoc rather than discuss and debate it as part of the process of public policy making.

That said, a country that doesn't understand its national interests is condemned to repeatedly act outside them. They are the foundation upon which foreign policies and diplomacy must be erected and resources expended. They are an expression of the inner us and the ambitions we harbour for ourselves in the world, butted up against the hard, cold realities of that world itself. Without a clear articulation of national interests, foreign policy may well become, in the words of the man to whom this volume is dedicated, diplomatic sage Allan Gotlieb, "arbitrary, quixotic or even a personal indulgence of its leader." Worse yet, it could degenerate into an exercise in communications spin that serves little more than the news cycle.

The first thing to be said about national interests is that they are not carved in the Canadian Shield. They are not immutable, but neither are they infinitely malleable. They are the product of political choices – better and worse choices, to be sure, and choices constrained by international power arrangements, geography and resources, domestic political circumstances, imagination, ambition, and perceptions of the intentions of others. Canada went to war alongside the United States in Korea, Kuwait, and Kosovo, but not in Vietnam or Iraq. Choices were made. During the Cold War, Finland managed its geographic proximity to the superpower next door quite differently than Canada did with regard to its superpower neighbour – for good reasons. The factors shaping these choices are perpetually in motion – sometimes evolving glacially and other times at warp speed, often discernible in the moment but periodically difficult to detect other than retrospectively. As facts on the ground change – oil replaces fur as the most valued commodity, Germany is pacified, the Soviet Union crumbles, China rises, groupings of ethnic Sikhs or Tamils or Ukrainians pursue external agendas – the need arises to rediscover where national interests lie. At the time of the Boer War in the 1890s and the First World War, most Canadians would have said they lay with the empire, although a vociferous minority disagreed. By the Second World War, King was trying to distance Canada from empire, but felt obliged to proceed, to borrow a phrase from critic F.R. Scott, not by halves but by quarters. The war confirmed the power shift already long underway, away from the kingdom across the pond toward the republic sprawled along our only land border. We adjusted our national interest compass accordingly.

Today, while few of common sense would challenge the primacy of the American relationship, historically significant global power shifts again impel us toward some form of recalibration. And so our intellectual elite, with Allan Gotlieb among them, struggle anew with questions that might have seemed settled or less urgent a decade or two ago with the collapse of communism and the advent of the free trade era with the United States.

It turns out Lord Palmerston was only half right. Nations may indeed have no permanent friends or allies, as he pronounced, but neither are their interests necessarily permanent either.

Thus the national interest is an iterative concept. As change in the world order has moved from the evolutionary to the explosive, old conceptions no longer serve us well. To muddy the waters further, any reconsideration must go beyond how we see our place within the world to include how we address the world within our place. The fact that the "we," in Canada's case, is also in the midst of a historic transformation makes the quest to identify the national interest more sensitive and complex. And all the more necessary, especially given that other players (the TSX, for instance) or ethnic population groups will seek to provide their own definition of the national interests. This is now a multiplayer game.

Furthermore, the realization of national interests, once identified, will not be manifest by destiny. They must be pursued through consistent, coherent, and focused strategies and policies. This can be accomplished only via skilled and persistent diplomacy, the act of relating to external nations (and non-state actors) in a manner that shapes outcomes to our liking. Pronouncements of the death of diplomacy in a digitally networked age are wildly off mark. In a world in which prairie fires of public opinion can suddenly consume policy makers and in which revolutions and genocides unfold in days, not years, the need for clearly articulated principles, preferably reflecting a political consensus, is all the more crucial.

A strong foreign policy rests on the twin principles of good preparation and strong relationships – both grounded in a broadly based understanding of a nation's goals and aspirations. The national interest is the springboard to playing an interdependent and fast-moving world well. The digital age does not diminish the value of diplomacy; it merely raises the costs and benefits of poor or good execution. This is doubly so in a country like Canada, a non–Great Power whose economic aspirations exceed its market grasp, and whose ties to the world are human as well as institutional.

We live in a moment of once-in-a-century change, most particularly but not solely tied to the rise of Asia and the relative decline of the twentieth century's great superpower, as the United States goes from creditor to debtor nation, and battens down the hatches in the face of shadowy enemies. As if these power shifts are not challenging enough, nations must also grapple with how to best manage the competition for natural resources and brainpower; the political and economic implications of climate change (particularly, in Canada's case, for a nation that both produces fossil fuels and possesses the second largest Arctic coastline in the world); the rise of innovation to the commanding heights of the global economy; and the decay of old multilateral systems before new ones can fully take their place. Sovereignty, though grasped tightly to the bosom, is far more relative than ever before. Just ask an indebted Greece, or the external victims of its fiscal profligacy. Or, for that matter, those sideswiped by lax U.S. economic stewardship.

How Canadians engage with these bumpy transitions requires understanding our goals and crafting a game plan. In other words: knowing the national interest.

Allan Gotlieb's professional life – and his own accounting of it – tells us much about national interest. His formal diplomatic career began in the engine room of Lester Pearson's 1950s foreign ministry and ended on the bridge with Brian Mulroney in 1989. Along the way, this self-professed realist became a guiding light for foreign policy conservatives who embraced his continental vision, his disdain for those who would raise values and norms to the heights of interests, and his Kissinger-esque spurning of anything that smacked of sentimentality.

His 2004 C.D. Howe Benefactors lecture, "Romanticism and Realism in Canada's Foreign Policy," delivered when he was seventy-six, produced the lion in winter's loudest roar. It is still widely cited by academics and practitioners as a tour de force, both for its insider's account of twentieth-century Canadian diplomacy and for its powerful argument in favour of a foreign policy heavily oriented to the United States. In the essay, he sliced and diced the values-laden school that distressed him ever since his earliest years as a legal officer on the highly functional Law of the Sea file, a policy he portrayed as having been of fundamental importance to the national interest but of marginal interest to a department hypnotized by the siren call of more post-Suez Nobel Peace Prize opportunities.

He used the lecture to decry an impulse in Canada's foreign policy "which drives us to try to export our values to the less fortunate people of the world" and to believe that other countries should emulate our values of multiculturalism, compassion, democracy, and tolerance. Amidst all this "value projection, peace building, and norm creation," he despaired that the national interest would fail to secure its proper place in policy making.

In fact, Gotlieb told me over lunch in his downtown Toronto law office, his entire career had been coloured by the view that our foreign policy lost its way post-Pearson as the country's various establishments (diplomatic, academic, journalistic) embraced the idea that Canada possessed a birthright to save less-exalted nations from their internal contradictions. "The national interest is the foundation of our foreign policy," Gotlieb said over a Spartan sandwich and water. "There has to be a purpose behind our diplomacy. How can you practise diplomacy without the broader view of what a country is trying to achieve?"

Gotlieb portrays himself as an outlier in his devotion to the serious business of advancing Canadian prosperity and unity. Somehow, though, he managed to rise to the top of his chosen vocation, becoming a highly regarded under-secretary of state for External Affairs and Canada's ambassador to the United States first for Trudeau and then Mulroney. The free trade negotiations provided the crowning achievement that has animated Gotlieb's intellectual work since leaving government. His C.D. Howe lecture reaffirmed his belief in the indispensability of the continental relationship and the need to deepen it even further in the wake of 9/11. For him, there are no counterbalancing policies, no Third Options, as Trudeau had proposed in the early 1970s in a spectacularly failed approach to reducing our reliance on the United States. For Gotlieb, realism hits the road along the forty-ninth parallel. The Americans dominated the world economy and lived within miles. There was no alternative. He was right.

In re-reading the lecture, it seems to me that the impressive subtlety of Gotlieb's own mind sometimes escaped him when it comes to his retrospective analysis. He does himself a disservice. The fact is that beneath his underlying contempt for "romanticism" in foreign affairs, Gotlieb is no unidimensional realist, but rather a pragmatic ecumenicist, including about 1970s-era Third Options. After all, there was nobody ready to pick up the slack and the U.S. was going strong. Although closely associated in the public mind with Mulroney's free trade agenda, Gotlieb also showers Trudeau with the highest of praise for his "realistic" insertion of national unity into the centre of Canadian foreign policy at a time when France was meddling in our domestic affairs. He's also a great admirer of Pearson's long tenure in the foreign ministry, most particularly for the coherence he brought by joining up the causes of interests and values. In Pearson, Gotlieb sees not a misbegotten romantic, but a straight-ahead realist who blended ambition for Canada's role in the world with the good sense to choose causes in which Canada and the United States were aligned, such as the Suez and Cyprus crises.

But it is hard to consider Pearson without thinking of values, peace building, and norms, alongside the realpolitik of his execution. After all, this is the man who inserted the so-called Canadian article into NATO's charter, committing signatories to improve themselves politically, socially, and economically. On closer examination, Gotlieb accords great respect in his C.D. Howe paper to those who worked to resolve conflicts in the Suez and Cyprus, and for those who invested in international institutions for a better world. "It is in the interests of Canadians to live in a stable and peaceful world," he comments. What is he speaking of here other than norms policed by international bodies? It may be that he prefers the World Trade Organization over the International Criminal Court, but at the end of the day, they're both in the same line of business, except for the obvious fact that one is embraced by the United States and one, at least for now, is not.

In May 1988, the real Gotlieb peeked through in a lecture at the University of Toronto. He spoke of a historical straight line that could be discerned in Canada's quest for independence and global engagement, and lauded the giants of the old External Affairs order for working "tirelessly, creatively, and ultimately successfully" to build a new international order. "They sought an order that assured Canadian security, preserved Canadian independence, and liberated Canadian aspirations."

I was struck by the phrase "liberated Canadian aspirations." It sounds straight out of the values and norms do-gooders phrase book.

If Gotlieb appreciates Pearson, but not those policies subsequently carried out under his banner, could it be that he is a seeker of a similarly balanced approach rather than a detractor of it? Let's remember his comment that the national interest is an expression of what a country is trying to achieve. This is not the language of determinism but rather a recognition of the roles that identity and aspirations play in national interest.

Perhaps what he really objects to is muddle – policies disconnected from a considered conception of a country's international purpose and comparative advantage. Indeed, he counselled me at the conclusion of our lunch, the less powerful and therefore more constrained a nation, the more attentive it must be to consistency, coherence, and the long term.

I had known Gotlieb in passing, but not well, before I took on the assignment from the Canadian International Council to chair its Global Positioning Strategy (GPS) panel. He was immediately discouraging. He pointed me to repeated arguments he had made over many years that foreign policy reviews were almost always a waste of time, if not a distraction. He assisted us nonetheless and promoted our results generously, even when they challenged some approaches with which he had been long associated.

Our panel explored the national interest question at each stop on a six-city tour of Canada. Were we on the right trajectory and, if not, what would be required to alter the trajectory on everything from relations with the United States and Asia to Arctic policy and the energy-and-environment nexus? We knew that anything and everything could reasonably be argued to fall within the national interest, as many were inclined to do, thus rendering it useless. As a result, we spoke about relative interests. Mexico, for instance, mattered more to Canada than Mauritius, the Arctic more than the Antarctic, knowledge trade more than trade in sealskins.

The jumping-off point for our analysis was the critical Canada-U.S. relationship. America's mountain of personal and public debt and the increasing polarization and infantilism of its political system concerned us. So too did the hardening of the border, through which a quarter of Canadian economic activity passed.

We were shocked when we crunched the numbers ourselves to find that while Canadian exports to the United States had grown by 350 per cent in the first dozen years after the free trade agreement, they had stalled thereafter. Worse yet, when you backed out energy exports, merchandise trade had actually dropped 20 per cent from 2000 to 2008. The "longest undefended border" conception with which most Canadians had grown up had apparently given way to what now was arguably the most heavily fortified border between advanced democracies.

The facts on the ground had changed markedly since the free trade era of the late twentieth century:

- The United States no longer provided a reliable engine for Canada's incremental growth, either from an economic or political point of view.
- Canada was still hugely vulnerable to economic shock from a border interruption. Therefore, we needed to find ways to deepen relations with the United States.
- At the same time, the national interest required Canada to broaden its relationships beyond the United States, particularly in Asia, but also with Mexico, Brazil, and others in our hemisphere.

In other words, the national interest demanded that Canada learn to walk and chew gum at the same time. We needed to be better friends with our best friend, and we needed more friends in the world. On both counts, Canada was falling short.

If the dawning of a multi-polar era and the self-inflicted wounds of U.S. policy meant that the national interest involved much more than simply securing greater access and selling more and more stuff to the United States, what exactly did it involve? Or, to put a Wayne Gretzky–like spin on it, where was the puck heading?

The puck was heading to Asia, of course. But Canada was stuck in its own zone, with nary a single free trade agreement across the Pacific, a disproportionately low share of trade and investment with China and India, and public perceptions of Canada as a Pacific nation actually receding between 2006 and 2010. All this despite the advantages of physical proximity (Vancouver is closer than Sydney to Beijing) and cultural familiarity (including 2.3 million

Chinese and Indo-Canadians, a cohort greater than the combined populations of Manitoba and Saskatchewan, or of the four Atlantic provinces combined).

Again, our policies lacked grounding within a national interest framework. They were ad hoc, highly politicized, and ever shifting, depriving them of long-term impact. For instance:

- The Harper government had continually snubbed China in its early years in office and continued to find opportunities to appeal to anti-China, pro-Taiwan elements.
- Canada had chosen to forsake participation in a budding political and economic grouping called the Trans-Pacific Partnership for fear it would upset the narrow and well-organized interests of the domestic dairy industry.
- Discussions about whether a pipeline might be built to carry synthetic crude from the oil sands for export across the Pacific were carried out by commercial interests alone.
- The attributes of Vancouver as arguably the most Asian city outside Asia had not attracted a strategy for building competitive advantage beyond improved transportation facilities.

Few would argue against greater engagement, but it failed to materialize in a concerted manner. Our GPS panel recommended building "a human bridge to Asia" that would promote the movement of people in a world of astounding labour mobility, particularly among global knowledge workers alongside goods, services, and capital. While government has failed to adequately leverage our pluralism for greater prosperity, the population has been building the bridge itself. This points to both the limits and strengths of government in a digital-age democracy: it lacks a monopoly over de facto policy making, yet it still has enough power over issues such as the control of borders, extradition treaties, and social security rules to enable or obstruct national interest policies.

For government, the issue is no longer simply brain gain or brain drain, but how to build a brain chain that would accommodate cross-pollinating population movements back and forth across the Pacific. Canada had been bold in recognizing China in 1970; the opportunity existed again for early mover advantage.

Nor did we seem to have a national interest strategy in mind for deepening relations with the United States. Nearly everyone, Gotlieb included, had grown skeptical of the political capacity of either Canada or the United States to implement some kind of Grand Bargain that would pull the countries closer together in economic and security matters. If a Grand Bargain wasn't on, or even if it was, how else could Canadian interests with the United States be advanced?

Our panel felt the answer lay in following the lead of Pearson (and Mulroney): be active in the world in a manner that satisfies the ambitions of Canada and is helpful to our allies. To some extent, we were already doing so in Haiti (although once again not using the occasion to maximum strategic advantage, for example, as a leverage point toward closer relations with Brazil). Either way, more policy meat and diplomatic resources were required. With Canada's Armed Forces nearing the end of their combat mission in Afghanistan, more public discussion was needed on how to utilize this well-trained national asset as a stabilization force elsewhere.

And so it went as one canvassed all the changes afoot. Our policies on innovation were outmoded. Our approach to the hemisphere was stop-go. Our defence policies were still more attuned to the protection of Canada, one of the least threatened land masses in the world, than to the protection of Canadians in an age of terrorism and mobility.

Arctic policy was similarly behind the times at a moment when the region was growing in geo-political significance, as global warming unlocked resources and rendered year-round shipping possible. There had been too much chest-beating about sovereignty and defence, and too little attention to economic and social development and environmental protection in this condominium atop the globe.

Canada dreamed up the Arctic Council in the 1990s and was its first chair. Then we melted into the background. But with proper leadership and ambition, this organization could be turned into a European Union of a highly interdependent North, charged with drafting a cooperative regimen of development and safety policies and providing a forum to ward off potential security misunderstandings. A small step in the direction of practical solutions was taken with a simple realistic logic in 2011 with a coordinated search-and-rescue policy among Arctic nations.

Such a definition of Canada's national interest in the north would certainly provide Canadians with a strong sense of purpose – holding out the promise to deliver greater prosperity, promote a more peaceful coexistence, and unify a broad spectrum of the population, aligning, in Gotlieb's appreciation of Pearson, "our idealistic goals and our basic national interest."

Now in his eighties, Gotlieb is still in motion. He remains an advocate for a Canada-U.S. relationship governed by a community of law rather than the caprice of Congressional politics. But, he doesn't want to bet the farm on it. In the introduction to a recent book called *Canada's Century*, he wrote that Washington's "unreformed entitlements and undisciplined borrowing are hobbling America's power to be a world leader," and warned about "Canada's prospects if we are so closely tied to an America with major economic problems." In his 2004 C.D. Howe lecture, Gotlieb demurred that "we cannot respond to the challenges with more Third Option–type practices." Today, he believes the Third Option's moment has finally arrived.

If the natsional interest is an iterative process involving making choices in changing circumstances, the time has come to chart a renewed national interest course. Purposefulness beats drift every time.

*With appreciation to Anouk Dey of the Canadian International Council, for her learned research assistance.

part four
diplomacy in the digital age

PROFESSIONALS AND AMATEURS IN THE DIPLOMACY OF THE AGE OF INFORMATION

Denis Stairs

We live in a breathless age. Technological change is (almost) everywhere. It's possible to tire of it. But even those who are mad as hell and don't want to take it anymore find they can't escape it. One of the consequences is the tendency to think we encounter a new watershed every day. We are told that even diplomacy, sometimes described as the second-oldest profession, will never be the same. The telegraph, telephone, short-wave radio, airplanes and air mail, CNN, the mechanics of globalization, the Internet, WikiLeaks, and, more generally, the new "social media" have each been heralded, in their turn, by the claim that they will finish off the traditional diplomatist.

Like most pronouncements of the sweeping sort, such assertions have the currency of the partial truth. Technological changes spawn other changes, too. But in politics, some realities – often the most fundamental ones – don't change much at all. If we are going to try to straighten out our understanding of these matters, therefore, we need to start with some analytical clarity. We don't have to be laborious about it, but we at least need to separate means from ends, techniques from substance, instruments from consequences, the how from the what.

For the purpose of this enterprise, and putting consular

activities to one side, it will be assumed here that diplomats and diplomacy are essentially concerned with three main functions: one, the acquisition and delivery of "intelligence," where intelligence is taken to include not merely factual information but also (and much more importantly) the careful analysis of its potential implications for both future developments abroad and decision making at home; two, the conduct of negotiations, often in the company of others, with the representatives of foreign powers; and three, the design and management of "public relations" activity aimed at nongovernmental publics, organized or otherwise, in other countries (and sometimes in the home environment, too). It will be convenient to consider each of these in turn.

The Intelligence Function

The central question here is whether the diplomat's traditional intelligence-gathering and analysis function has been rendered somehow redundant by the arrival of the latest information technologies.

It is easy to make the case. Ambassadors everywhere have been defending themselves for decades against the charge that the ease and speed of communications and the proliferation of electronic news media have diminished both their own freedom of manoeuvre and the utility of their intelligence assessments. Canada's Prime Minister Pierre Trudeau once famously complained that he found the contents of the *New York Times* more useful than the submissions he received from officials in the Department of External Affairs. He seems later to have softened his opinion. But the idea has long legs.

Currently, Prime Minister Stephen Harper's disdain for the advice of the Foreign Service has become a matter of common knowledge, in his case reputedly compounded by his belief that DFAIT is a nesting place for views that are not "in alignment" (as the current jargon has it) with the position of his government. The compounding effect of such distrustful presumptions of partisanship was similarly evident long ago in Prime Minister John Diefenbaker's dismissive description of senior Foreign Service officers as "Pearsonalities." Implicit in both the Harper and Diefenbaker examples is the premise that the advice of the Foreign Service is rooted less in evidence drawn from professional expertise than in normative or ideological precepts that can make it irrelevant to a government operating from different starting assumptions. Thus defined, the divide between the amateurs in the political leadership and the professionals in the public service is not professional, but political.

Ironically, the recent WikiLeaks release of communications between American embassies and the U.S. State Department can easily be interpreted as adding grist to the argument that the professionals have little of value to offer. This is because the predominant feature of the leaks is not that they lead to genuine revelation – that they let out "secrets" – but that they're so predictable. With occasional exceptions – most of them factoids – their contents are pretty much what moderately attentive observers would expect. A day or so in advance of the first of the major WikiLeaks releases, Secretary of State Hillary Clinton initiated a series of apologetic "damage control" calls to a number of her counterparts abroad. She later reported in an interview that a foreign minister in the Middle East reacted with a laughing comment to the effect that she shouldn't worry: "You should hear what we say about you!" Clinton took the rejoinder in good part, and clearly felt Americans at large should do the same. If her account of the exchange is accurate, the obvious conclusion is that both parties were reasonably confident that neither of them would be taken aback by the views and assessments that were circulating in the ministry of the other.

If moderately attentive independent observers are not very surprised by what classified diplomatic communications of recent vintage are found to contain, and if insider professionals in other countries are unlikely to be surprised by them either, perhaps little is added by diplomatic reporting after all, particularly since the flow of parallel communications in publicly accessible media is now so massive and conveyed in close to "real" time.

But of course this argument is no more than superficially persuasive. In 1996 Prime Minister Jean Chrétien was reputed to have pressed for a Canadian initiative in Zaire in response to a television news report of horrendous slaughter and starvation. To the extent that the idea was conceived in compassion, it was an admirable impulse. But for a variety of reasons, of which the professionals were well aware, it was hopelessly impracticable, and ended in embarrassment. Again, in 2006, Canada escalated its involvement in Afghanistan by taking on a substantial combat role in Kandahar. Those who made the decision, however, appear to have done so more for ancillary diplomatic purposes than because they were in a position to reach an informed judgment on the viability of the mission itself. That this was the case was a reflection in large measure of the government's lack of knowledgeable diplomatic and other sources of intelligence in the field. Since then, government authorities have come to know more – much more – but the school in which they have acquired their learning has been a school of hard knocks. Ask the army.

The reality, in short, is not that operating in a world enveloped by electronic information makes diplomatic intelligence redundant. The reality is that it makes it even more necessary, albeit in some respects even more difficult to generate in reliably finished form.

For this there are many explanations, some of them easily discerned. Perhaps the most important is that the other purveyors of potentially pertinent information – and they are both plentiful and diverse – are not charged with doing the government's job. Most of them will not have the interests of Canada and its citizenry in mind. The vast majority will not be thinking of Canada at all. Even individual Canadians who work abroad for businesses or nongovernmental organizations, while in some respects important and certainly expert sources of reportage, are nonetheless private actors. They lack the government perspective. Their agendas are their own and their focus is narrow. By contrast, the governmental agenda, both at home and abroad, is wider and more multidimensional. The government always has a variety of often-conflicting considerations to take into account. It therefore has to make trade-offs, and in so doing to have at least a rough grasp of the costs and benefits of the alternative policy mixes on offer. In making foreign policy, a sense of context is required. The strengths and weaknesses of competing opinions and arguments have to be weighed. The potential for second- and third-order consequences has to be calculated. The possible and the impossible (from the government's perspective) have to be separated. Priorities have to be identified before agendas are set.

This, clearly, is a multifaceted process. Multiple levels, departments, and agencies of government may be involved in it. But in more cases than not, and especially in the "high stakes" cases, the assessments of the Foreign Service will be – and certainly they should be – at the centre of the argument. Those who leave them out do so at their peril. If they do, they are much more likely to make high-stakes errors.

Prime Minister Trudeau's approval of the *New York Times* implied that much of this analytical job, along with the task of separating wheat from chaff, can be accomplished simply by consulting the conventional media, and, most notably, the quality press. But while the agendas of the press are prominently positioned among the influences affecting the agendas of government, the two are far from identical, and the considerations that guide newspaper editors and television producers are notoriously indifferent to the distinction between what merely catches the eye and what really matters. If the reporters and those who direct them, moreover, are primarily obligated to employers and audiences outside Canada (as in significant degree they are), the interests and agendas they have in mind will not – except by happenstance – be those of Canadians.

Nor can this problem easily be solved, in practice at any rate, by stationing Canadian correspondents abroad. As impressive as many of these correspondents are, posting them in other countries is a very expensive undertaking. In consequence, there are too few of them, and they have too much territory to cover. While the reports of the conventional media are important inputs into the analytical process, and while they can help government analysts develop their own agendas, they are simply one part of the mix, and cannot be a substitute for the contributions of informed officials.

A second reason for arguing that the intelligence-analysis function more than ever requires the attention of the diplomatic professionals is inherent in the first. It, too, is a by-product of the pervasive (and *in*vasive) growth of communications technology. Its substance can be summed up in the popular cliché: "If you build it, they will come." Collectively we have constructed a phenomenal communications system that carries extraordinary volumes of "data" at very high speed and relatively low cost. Some who access the system appear to feel that it empowers them, even when it doesn't. Others clearly think they can exploit it to ensure that they get more than their allotted fifteen minutes of fame. Whatever the motivation, the result is clear. We face not too little information, but too much. The concept of "information overload" was at one time a clever exaggeration and it drew attention to a developing trend. But now the trend is a torrent. It threatens to weigh us down. And it can't be beaten back. It has to be dealt with, coped with, lived with.

In the pursuit of foreign affairs, this means that the task of separating what really matters from what doesn't is as essential as ever. But it's also more difficult than ever. As specialists in intelligence like to put it, the "signals" have to be extracted from the "noise." The problem is that there is a lot more noise around. If the job is to be done reliably, efficiently, and economically, it is best done by those who know not only what to look for in the field, but also what the folks at home most need to understand if they are to make their decisions wisely. Sometimes the task is straightforward, but often not. Political leaderships can be talented assessors of their domestic constituencies and how to work with them. If they aren't, they can hire people who are. But in neither category are observers with a nuanced understanding of the politics of Egypt, or Iraq, or Afghanistan, or Libya, or Rwanda, or Zaire in plentiful supply. The press can give them an inkling. A good book can impart some expertise. But few in high office have the time or inclination to read such books. Someone has to distill the essentials for them. Intelligence analysts therefore come into play, and in the making of foreign policy, Foreign Service is (or ought to be) at the centre of the analytical action.

It is worth noting *en passant* that the challenge of this distillation process has been greatly intensified in recent decades not only because of the overload of *international* information, but also because of the more general growth of information that has to be taken into account. The wishes of the neo-cons notwithstanding, governments are getting bigger because they have more demands to meet and more issues to process. That in itself is a side effect of technological progress, the advance of information technology included. In the modern world, to point to the most obvious example, autarchies are long gone. Financiers misbehave on Wall Street, and economies around the world feel the pain. Governments, even if led by those who loudly proclaim that minimal governance and free markets are best, are forced to intervene, and they have to do so in tandem with their counterparts abroad. But this means that last-say decision makers have a great deal to think about. The overcrowding of their agendas leads relentlessly to the demand for one-page memos, double-spaced, with bulleted noun phrases where nuanced paragraphs once used to be.

To repeat, in such a world – busy, crowded, and noisy – the requirement for distillation can't be ducked. But it's much harder than it was in simpler and slower-moving times.

For this, too, political leaders need diplomats, even if they think they don't.

There is another reason why the field experience of seasoned diplomats and their textured understanding of politics in foreign jurisdictions, as well as in international institutions of various kinds, are becoming more crucial to effective intelligence analysis. Policy communities are at once helped and bedeviled by the explosion in the volume of communications they receive and the distracting "noise" that accompanies it. In addition, however, both they and their political constituencies now run a much greater risk than before of being persuasively influenced by calculated disinformation. This is not in itself a new phenomenon, but the Internet and its social media offshoots have opened up extraordinary new vehicles for purveying mischicvously misleading messages – messages that can be directed to carefully chosen targets of varying size. The origins of such messages, moreover, can easily be disguised. Ordinary Internet users need considerable experience before they become adept at detecting cleverly concealed spam, and even nerdy veterans are occasionally fooled. One of the newer educational tasks of universities is to ensure that students learn to bring the same critical cast of mind to bear on what they find on the Internet as they were traditionally taught to apply to the books and journals they are expected to read.

The stakes are high in education. They can be a great deal higher in international affairs, however, as the round of copycat rebellions in North Africa and the Middle East has recently demonstrated. If disinformation campaigns come into play in contexts such as these, the diplomats on the spot are likely to be among the few who are well suited to sniffing them out. The spin doctors who inhabit the Prime Minister's Office and the political aides of other members of the Cabinet should be among the first to understand the danger, and to recognize that its manifestations may not be detected unless knowledge-able minds are on watch.

The world of foreign affairs, a world more complex and multidimensional than ever before, has thus become crowded with noisy and increasingly intrusive amateurs. Given their other responsibilities and interests, many of them cannot escape their amateurism. Such realities make (or should make) the voice of the diplomatic professionals more crucial than ever to the development of sound foreign policy.

The negotiating function

A recurring attack on the diplomatic service over the years has been founded on the observation that the international agenda is increasingly focused on issues, many of them tech-nically complex, that fall within the mandates of other depart-ments, agencies, and levels of government. This has always been true in at least some degree, but we are now far beyond the era in which diplomacy was preoccupied only with secu-rity, empire, and the flow of commerce. Almost every govern-ment apparatus has acquired an interest in foreign affairs and policy preferences to match. Some have developed special-ized staffs to pursue them. The Department of Foreign Affairs and International Trade is sometimes regarded by this grow-ing band of interlopers as helpful, and recently it has been responding to a sense of being out of political favour by adver-tising itself within the bureaucracy as a kind of "service" department, as if its motto were: "Have negotiators. Will travel." But DFAIT is also commonly viewed elsewhere in the bureaucracy as an obstacle to getting things done and as a source of tiresome procrastination and delay. If the issues are very complex, the generalists who predominate in the Foreign Service may need time to be brought up to speed. In important bilateral contexts – the relationship with the United States being the most obvious example – the DFAIT agenda may be cluttered with issues that lead it to focus on other priorities, or may be concerned about timing and other tactical calculations in a way that prevents the department that leads on the substance from getting on with its job.

While he was under-secretary of state for External Affairs, Allan Gotlieb became so concerned about this problem and the need for a coordinated approach to the conduct of foreign affairs that he urged Prime Minister Trudeau to designate the DEA as a "central agency" (like the Privy Council Office, Finance, and the Treasury Board). The prime minister bought the argument and sold it to the Cabinet. But it was hard to make it stick. The PCO controlled the gateway to the Cabinet. Finance controlled the supply of resources. The Treasury Board had a lot to say about how the resources could be spent. In bureaucratic environments, these are substantial assets and they confer real power. DFAIT, by contrast, had only its powers of persuasion and the prime minister's general endorsement with which to defend its orchestrating ambitions.

The struggle is with us still. Most recently it has been represented by the attempt to emphasize interdepartmental co-operation in responding to crises in fragile or failed states ("whole-of-government" operations, and all that). Even, however, in such relatively well-defined contexts – presumably rendered especially compelling by the spurts of death and destruction that accompany them – progress has been extremely slow. Bureaucratic silos don't like bridges.

But the power of Mr. Gotlieb's case does not depend on high-drama examples alone. In their absence, his argument would still be stronger now than when he first made it. This is because both the number and variety of interlopers in the conduct of foreign affairs continue to increase as the international agenda widens, and as electronic communications become more pervasive. This process, again, has had a very long history, but it was accelerated in the post–World War II period, first, by citizens who were dismayed by the threat of nuclear war and, second, by those who rebelled against the war in Vietnam. It can be argued, however, that the birth of the current version of the phenomenon really began with the 1972 Stockholm Conference on the Environment. The conference was not concerned with a "statist" security issue in the traditional sense, although it later came to be framed as one, but it was regarded by attentive environmentalists as extremely urgent, and it had potential implications for a wide array of interests inside government and out. Many delegations – the Canadian prominently among them – were eclectically composed in ways that reflected the variety of the stakes involved.

Since then, nongovernmental players have been increasingly evident at international conferences. Sometimes they have even enjoyed seats at the table, or very close to it. From time to time they have succeeded in bringing governmental initiatives to a dead stop. On occasion, too, they have been the source of constructively innovative ideas and have played significant roles in the politics and diplomacy through which such ideas have been put into effect.

In the end, however, there is no escaping the need – even

in so transnationalized an age – for state action. Crudely put, states have the authority to regulate. They also have the authority to tax. Other players – NGOs, private corporations, think tanks, and the like – can exercise influence. If well-resourced and effectively coordinated in multiple jurisdictions, they can exercise a *lot* of influence. But having influence and having authority are not the same, and in international affairs, the states, along with the organizations they construct for themselves, are still the custodians of the latter. The representatives of states are thus left, as in centuries past, with the final negotiating responsibility. The difference is that the negotiators now have to deal with the private players as well as with their governmental counterparts.

Once again, it bears repeating that this is not a new phenomenon. Diplomacy has long been a two-level game. But in recent decades, negotiating with domestic constituencies has become a much more intrusive part of the process, and it makes the diplomatic task far more difficult. It can even make it impossible. Not everyone can do it. Politicians can help, partly by recognizing their "accountability" and taking the heat. Representatives of other departments and levels of government can help, too. Among other things, they usually know their own constituencies best. Nonetheless, in complex multilateral environments especially, there is no escaping the need for the professionals. The job they do takes practice.

The public relations function

Here, too, the function itself is far from new, although line diplomats have tended over the years to be ill at ease in the face of public relations. Their traditional comfort zone was with their counterparts abroad or with other representatives of the governments to which they were assigned. Increasingly over the twentieth century, carefully fostered relationships with non-governmental elites, not least of all in the business, journalistic, cultural, and other opinion-leading communities were also assumed to be helpful. But other potentially useful targets – including politicians who were not holding office in the executive branch of the government – were normally approached in circumspect style, and general publics were assumed in many cases to lie beyond the pale. If they were targeted at all, the task was often assigned to "information" agencies (propaganda agencies in all but name), or were relegated to operators (for example, short-wave radio broadcasters) organizationally situated at some remove from the diplomatic service. Addressing local constituencies over the heads of the host government was thought in most cases to be ill advised. It could get in the way of opportunities for constructive diplomatic conversation. If there were exceptions, they tended to be of the innocuously ceremonial or hospitality sort.

The first senior Canadian diplomat to break with the traditional mould was Allan Gotlieb in the context of the relationship with the United States. It was a strategic decision, reflecting both the peculiarities of the American system of government and the extraordinary range of issues on the Canada-U.S. agenda. The functional interconnections between the two countries meant that decisions taken on one side of the border often had significant repercussions, by accident, if not on purpose, on the other. In these circumstances, and given the separation-of-powers system, the Canadian interest could hardly be promoted adequately by concentrating on the State Department alone, or even on the whole of the Executive Branch. In executive-dominant parliamentary systems, it might be both courteous and sensible for diplomats to leave the legislative branch of the host government alone. But in the United States, protecting Canadian interests required a more pervasively interventionist strategy, albeit sensitively and discreetly managed. Not only key players in the Congress, but also the governments of many of the individual states, along with strategically chosen nongovernmental actors, needed to be targeted. The task might range from simple "education" to the cultivation of tactical alliances grounded in common interests. In so pluralistic a polity, with so much diffusion of power, the pursuit of vested interest is a lobbying enterprise above all. Diplomats in Washington would have to be lobbyists, too.

With the deepening of the integration process and the transnationalizing of issues almost everywhere, similar requirements, as Gotlieb anticipated, are becoming increasingly evident in other jurisdictions as well, and with the proliferation of voices on the Internet, the salient targets are now even more plentiful and diverse. Hence Evan Potter's emphasis on the need for a comprehensive "public diplomacy" strategy for Canada, and Daryl Copeland's far-reaching argument in support of what he has called "guerrilla diplomacy."

But these sorts of tasks cannot safely be assigned to personnel who lack a diplomat's sense of their context and purpose and a nuanced understanding of the attitudes and predilections of the targeted communities. Once again, the requirements amplify the importance of what a diplomat presumably has to offer, while at the same time intensifying the challenge it entails.

To all this can be added one final reminder: many of the most successful and constructive initiatives in the conduct of Canadian foreign policy have emanated from the Foreign Service. Among the most far reaching were ones that profoundly influenced the United Nations Conference on the Law of the Sea. They were moulded in impressive measure by the diplomat in whose honour this collection of essays has been written. They constituted a massively constructive contribution to the world order. More self-interestedly for Canada, they resulted in the largest expansion of the exploitable territory of any state by peaceful means in the history of international affairs.

The enterprise could not have been conceived by amateurs. It would never have been formulated in the Prime Minister's Office.

CORPORATE DIPLOMACY IN THE INFORMATION AGE:
Catching Up to the Dispersal of Power

George Haynal

I was Allan Gotlieb's executive assistant thirty years ago. Back then, we knew what was what and who was who. We thought we had a good fix on the future. In the 1980s, international relations were fully the domain of sovereign states (some more sovereign than others) and they were managed by "diplomats," a global guild of public servants. The rules of the game were clear. The Cold War meant that all the world's major security concerns were played out on one chessboard. Every state knew its place, either on one side or the other of the great divide or, in the case of the non-aligned, playing both ends against the middle. There was also an identifiable centre to world economic affairs, and it was the North Atlantic. The rules and codes of behaviour of the Organisation for Economic Co-operation and Development (OECD) characterized, at least nominally, the behaviour of well over two thirds of the world economy. There were economies that mattered, because they played a real role in world trade and multilateral rule making, and many more that did not, among which were China and important members of the "non-aligned." Economics were a subset of the great strategic conflict, with markets and rules divided along ideological lines.

Civil society was in its infancy, poorly understood, poorly organized, without the technological means to assert itself as a force in the conduct of the world's business.[1] Corporations, too, had only an indirect role in international affairs.

Even the so-called multinationals were really national in character, closely identified with a few home jurisdictions, almost all of which were members of the G-7. Corporations with international operations used "their" governments to exert international influence on their behalf. States did this through the pursuit of rules-based open systems for trade and investment but also, often enough, major governments deployed (and still deploy) raw power abroad to serve their corporations' agendas. With the exception of the extractive resource sectors that were de facto global, their investments were focused on OECD economies (the OECD was then largely a club of more or less like-minded liberal democracies). In other jurisdictions, they were engaged principally as suppliers of consumer and industrial manufactures, including armaments.

Other than in small mono-economies, where they actually owned the country's export resource (minerals or bananas, for example), and with the possible exception of the Seven Sisters oil companies elsewhere, even the largest multinationals lacked the essential element of what would eventually give them real international power: the ability to invest around the world, largely as they wished.

Unknown to us, or at least to me then, the world was on the verge of revolutionary change. Two historic and entwined phenomena – the deconstruction of the Cold War order and the disintermediation of institutions by democratizing information technology – have been reshaping society, the state, the economy, and the power relationships among them, for almost three decades. This period of creative destruction is far from over, and the order that it will eventually produce is far from clear.

What is clear is that we are now in the second phase of this revolutionary process. The first saw the empowerment of corporations at the expense of the state in both the western world and in what were formerly centrally planned economies. In the former, the state changed its focus from invigilating the economy to partnering with it. In the latter, the state gave up complete control to become the national economy's part owner and patron. In both, however, elites continued to be in confident command.

The second phase of this revolution is now in full flight, diminishing the power of the state and of corporations, as well as of the traditional elites which serve and rely on both. A technologically empowered Demos, sometimes sufficiently organized to constitute civil society, sometimes a promiscuous, episodic, and anarchic expression of will by unaccountable individuals and entities – as well as a parallel global criminal economy, and terrorist networks – is asserting itself in powerful, sometimes dramatic, and unpredictable ways. Both the opportunities for corporations and the risks they face have become more complicated as a result.

The case for corporate diplomacy

Corporations are now free to be global

Technologically enabled value chains allow corporations to source their inputs virtually without regard to location, and to manage their marketing and distribution on a global basis.[2]

International trade and investment rules, negotiated by governments, perhaps without a full sense of the eventual implications, help protect corporations' right to do so. They can shift production across jurisdictions, invest in high value activities in the most congenial environments.[3] Rather than seeking corporate concessions for the right to invest, most states are now actively competing to attract and retain foreign direct investment (FDI). Corporations, therefore, now consider that they have a right to judge (and thus to take a role in shaping) policies that bear on their investment decisions. They now have the power to partner with rather than just to obey the state. This may look like corporate licence, and some corporations undoubtedly abuse it, but things are not so simple.

With independence comes responsibility

While state regulation may have eased in OECD economies, legitimate corporations still need equitable rules and effective rule making to plan and compete. Even without being obliged by regulators, they still need to maintain good governance to be sustainable, particularly if they are operating on a global basis, including in markets where standards of governance are lower than those that they are expected to meet in their home jurisdictions. More judicious corporations, conscious of the long term, also foster strong environmental practices from a sense of self interest (for example, because lean manufacture is not just cleaner, it is also more efficient) and are taking an interest in broader social issues for the same reasons. Their need for stability, for instance, is best served by equitable social structures rather than divided and unstable ones. Universal education provides a better and more sophisticated workforce. Reasonable levels of public health provide for a more reliable pool of labour; clean systems of government impose fewer "taxes" – official or otherwise – than corrupted ones. Stronger social and political environments, in short, lower the risks facing corporations and raise the returns from their investments. Fostering them, therefore, is not just a matter of public duty but of hard self-interest.

But even less-enlightened firms are now being obliged to accept new responsibilities – ones imposed by public opinion which has been empowered by information technology to exert ever more effective disciplines on corporate behaviour.

Civil society as regulator: co-opting corporations in the drive for global rules of behaviour

Technologically empowered civil society adds an increasingly significant new level of regulation to the corporate environment. Corporate behaviour is now scrutinized minute by minute, and subject to "enforcement" in many forms, including shareholder activism, legal challenges, media exposure, and political pressure. Corporate response to these challenges is complex because civil society is by definition heterogeneous. It makes multiple, sometimes conflicting demands for what is deemed appropriate corporate behaviour, in diverse environments, and presses issues that are sometimes beyond corporate control.

The sum of these demands is, in effect, that corporations should export not just goods and capital, but also norms of conduct that reflect the mores of their home jurisdictions.

Exporting values as part of doing business can be a powerful instrument for advancing Western values in the world (and can coincide with corporate interest in ensuring that there is a level global playing field), but it presents a difficult practical challenge for individual corporations, competing with players from emerging economies in which "business" and "development" are often still seen as two sides of the same coin and the line between state and corporation is opaque. These emerging-market competitors and their governments do not necessarily play, or wish to play, by our rules either in their home markets (where corporations are often instruments of public policy) or in third markets, particularly those with weak governance.[4] The need to meet these conflicting competitive demands is going to keep driving corporations to adjust the balance in their relationship with rule makers and to press for global disciplines that apply equally to their emerging-market competitors.

The rise of the Demos and unpredictability: corporations must adapt their diplomacy

The near-global spread of broadband has given the Demos outside advanced democracies the capacity to organize and with that, the power to shame, discipline, constrain, and at the extreme, to destabilize, destroy, and potentially transform the state and the institutions on which business has relied to conduct its affairs.[5]

The Obama campaign and the Tea Party both provide powerful examples of how the Demos finds expression in developed democratic societies. But in societies without strong democratic institutions, discontent takes a radically different form. Unable to express itself through legitimate representative institutions, it is driven to seek the overthrow of the established order. This potential for radical instability presents corporations with unparalleled risk, and poses a diplomatic challenge of a scale and immediacy that few corporations can be expected to have anticipated. They need to cope in the immediate, but also look to the long term, which requires them to seek a place in the discourse where the future of such unstable systems is to be shaped.

Global value chains are a blessing, but also a source of vulnerability which corporations have no option but to try to manage

An additional motive driving corporations to assume increased responsibility for the public good but also to seek effective cooperation with governments is their intense reliance on global value chains.

The ability to organize business globally and on the basis of comparative advantage is a great benefit to business, but the vulnerability created by global operations also presents a new and intense level of risk. Global value chains are fragile. They rely not just on a high level of technological connectivity, but also on the capacity of large numbers of collaborators from heterogeneous environments to share in managing risk. Given the exponential growth of global value chains, the infrastructure on which they rely is already vulnerable to overload. But it is also exposed to disruption due to weather, terrorism, crime, and political interference. Multinationals are obliged to take on more responsibility for ensuring the efficient operation of value chains – the construction, maintenance, and operation of infrastructure, the protection of cargo and data – in areas that had previously been the domain of states. But the challenge is too complex for corporations to manage alone. They rely on the state for protection (against terrorism, piracy, cyber crime), investment (for infrastructure), as well as global rule making (to ensure property rights as well as the efficient rules around logistics management).

National identity is sometimes, but not always, a strength

While international trade and investment rules have helped make corporations mobile, there are still important sectors in important markets where only domestic players are allowed to participate (think Buy America and other less overt instances). Corporations look to international agreements to break down the barriers eventually, but have to cope on their own in the short term. This they often do by adopting global as well as multinational identities, establishing themselves as national corporations where this is the requirement for entry (GM, for instance, does not look to international trade reform to help sell cars in China). A global brand, independent of national identity, is also critical for global corporations, not just to ensure an appropriate recognition for their product, but also to insulate them from situations where national policies put their home and host governments in conflict. Building and maintaining such a brand is a major challenge for corporations' public diplomacy.

The theory and practice of corporate diplomacy in the new environment

The global corporation of 2011 is, in sum, not your grandfather's company. It has power and responsibilities that arc over political borders. Its interests are far more complex, as are its vulnerabilities. It is an actor in the international system alongside, no longer fully subservient to, states. It needs to manage its brand in multiple and sometimes conflictive environments. Its behaviour is under scrutiny from multiple constituencies as well as national and international regulators. Its global operations open it to unprecedented logistical risks. Instability in political systems lays it open to risks that are as difficult to manage as they are to anticipate. It has a continuing interest in maintaining maximum autonomy but is obliged to assume some responsibility for the global commons which, in turn, requires building new relationships with both states and civil society. It needs, in short, to practise structured diplomacy.

How do corporations do diplomacy?

Diplomacy begins with "foreign" policy:

• the articulation of vital interests;
• the identification of vulnerabilities;
• and the strategic deployment of instruments to pursue the former and compensate for the latter.

On the ground, it is expressed through six functions:

• the construction and maintenance of networks of influence;
• the generation of intelligence (purposeful information, not necessarily covert);
• the interpretation of realities across cultures and systems;

- branding, that is, the creation of a positive predisposition among decision makers and those who influence them;
- the negotiation of arrangements that prescribe mutually satisfactory behaviour;
- and conflict avoidance, management, and resolution.

All global corporations conduct these activities to one degree or another, but they are not often understood or managed as a coherent whole. Nor is their diplomacy yet fully attuned to the need to assume a more engaged role in management of the global commons. They need to manage relations with not only the state, but also the Demos, and to do so not just in a few like-minded national contexts, but in multiple and heterogeneous environments, all within an unsettled and mutating global system. Corporations need, in other words, to develop and practise comprehensive foreign policy.

The practice of corporate diplomacy also needs systematization. In the past, it was often episodic and unstructured. It focused largely on securing state support (in the form of subsidies, requests for regulatory and tax relief, favourable trade rules, and international sales promotion), and was conducted at high levels on a personal, often on a face-to-face, basis.

Sometimes the maintenance of relations with governments was delegated to associations, or subcontracted to outside lobbyists. Other functions that are properly part of a diplomatic toolkit were dispersed within the corporation. Public relations, regulatory, legal, environmental, strategic human resource, and international nodes often operated alongside and at the service of "real" business units rather than acting as integrated participants in strategic and tactical decision making.

The assessment of risk was not always informed by an

understanding of the broader environment. There was little ongoing dialogue on broader issues of policy with governments – think of the shibboleth "the business of Business is business."

International operations were either managed by expatriates with little connection to the corporation, or by rising executives being trained for higher-level responsibility, in most cases with little decentralization in decision making or risk management.

Reach out, get in touch, and internalize the externalities

Things are changing, but the world is changing faster. There is both the need and the room for more sophisticated corporate diplomacy. Corporate leaders need to have access to the broader environment, and to engage in a more systematic way with those who shape it.

Most corporations recognize the need to cultivate purposeful networks of knowledgeable and connected people. These networks need to be truly global, enabling the corporation to partner with powers, both public and private, that broadly share its interests, but they are particularly important in cultures where friendship and trust matter more than do contracts.

What corporations are coming to recognize is that these networks must reach beyond established elites. Corporate leaders have sometimes been seduced into believing that they understand foreign societies uniquely by dint of their friendship with "Davos Man," a representative of foreign elites whom they meet in international forums or through other social or educational interactions. This illusion of connection with foreign environments can be dangerous. Some members of local elites are "global" because they are connected to their peers around the world in the same measure that they are disconnected from their own societies. They are as likely to be surprised by the "street" as foreigners are. Others might be more global in the way they present themselves internationally than in their behaviour at home, using a global veneer to spin domestic realities for international audiences. Following the advice of such heterogeneous elites cannot be the only way to manage political or systemic risk in emerging and other nontraditional markets. Getting beyond overreliance on elite interaction is no easy matter, as even states are finding, but unlike corporations, states have always gone to considerable effort to maintain relations with those in opposition, those who stood as alternative, perhaps future, holders of power. Corporations need to devise ways of developing such relationships. Social media present opportunities for this sort of interaction with those outside the penumbra of established power. Corporations may be used to dealing with the people and the structures they know, but they need to enter into this virtual world in more than token fashion if they are to have a voice in the discourse on issues that affect them.

Social involvement under the umbrella of corporate social responsibility also offers avenues for real relationships with broadly representative layers in diverse societies. Corporations could fruitfully embrace the example of Western NGOs whose direct engagement with the less privileged allows them an understanding of social dynamics that often elude even governments, especially in nondemocratic societies.

Corporations also need to develop their own global people, building a leadership with international experience and knowledge, supported as may be required, by independent advisers. They need real local presence wherever they operate to help them understand the environment and to manage political risk. This requires a cadre of informed and loyal "ambassadors" closely connected to the decision-making level who can be deployed in critical jurisdictions to provide professional representation of their interests and informed advice on the local context within a framework of global strategy.

While these ambassadors might inevitably be focused on maintaining elite networks, corporations can also draw on the active social engagement of their less senior employees. Their own relationships within society should be fostered and their knowledge be made available as part of corporate decision making at the strategic as well as the day-to-day managerial level.

Most important, the net of international operations cannot be kept at arm's length from head office. The centre of corporate decision making must have on its staff an international corps, able to bring into everyday operations a cultural awareness of all the systems in which the corporation operates, and in particular to help it manage the multiplying risks that it faces, operating across many jurisdictions in a global environment whose shape and rules are not yet stable.

Conclusion

The global environment for business is mutating. Power and authority is dispersing beyond the structures on which business has historically relied. The changing environment demands an ever more systematic corporate diplomacy. The story, of course, is far from over. The disintermediation of the state and of the institutions that have provided the framework for the global economy continues apace. Global corporations have to run faster just to stand still, and faster still if they are to help shape their own future, rather than have it thrust upon them.

Notes

1   Civil society refers to the aggregate of non-governmental organizations and institutions that manifest interests and will of citizens; individuals and organizations in a society which are independent of the government (Dictionary.com's Twenty-first Century Lexicon).

2   A value chain is the sequential set of primary and support activities that an enterprise performs to turn inputs into value-added outputs for its external customers. As developed by Michael E. Porter, it is a connected series of organizations, resources, and knowledge streams involved in the creation and delivery of value to end customers. Value systems integrate supply-chain activities, from determination of customer needs through product/service development, production/operations and distribution, including (as appropriate) first-, second-, and third-tier suppliers. The objective of value systems is to position organizations in the supply chain to achieve the highest levels of customer satisfaction and value while effectively exploiting the competencies of all organizations in the supply chain (Ventureline.com).

3   Many markets in fact remain protected, including through the use of nontariff barriers such as regulatory particularisms. Corporations cope with protected markets in different ways, including through the establishment of "national" operations.

4   I speak to the general situation. Many corporations from emerging economies operate with high standards of governance, and often enough, established multinationals have been complicit in corruption and abuse of human rights and the environment. The difference remains however. OECD corporations can be "shamed" into acceptable behaviour because regulators, shareholders, media, and activists in their home jurisdictions have the means to do so, while firms from most emerging economies as of yet face much less compelling disciplines.

5   The fall of authoritarian regimes in North Africa at the hands of Internet-organized civil society has brought an interesting new kind of corporate player – the for-cause corporation (including Facebook and Google) – into the political realm.

OF SATRAPS AND SUPPLICANTS:
The Diplomatic Diary as the Last Safe Haven

Andrew Cohen

It is the winter of 1982, and Allan Gotlieb, the newly arrived ambassador of Canada to the United States, is making a round of courtesy calls on the proconsuls and panjandrums of Washington. On February 8 he visits Tip O'Neill, the Speaker of the House of Representatives, who was elected to Congress in 1952. Gotlieb is ushered into a marbled chamber of the Capitol, where he joins a clutch of other self-conscious peti-tioners awaiting an audience with the third man in line for the presidency. The stocky, pug-nosed O'Neill shambles in and works the room, pressing the flesh like the seasoned ward-heeler from Irish Boston that he is. Gotlieb introduces him-self, even though he'd met O'Neill at lunch the day before, assuming correctly that O'Neill won't remember him. *Well, why would he?* Their second meeting is brief and inconse-quential, without foreplay, pleasure, or climax; it lasts all of thirty seconds. "This was one of the more ludicrous encoun-ters in my diplomatic career," Gotlieb writes in his diary. "Some congressmen behave as if they are great satraps whose role it is to receive petitions from supplicants – and sometimes gifts as well."

As the ambassador would learn, politicians would often act like satraps around him. So too would the legions of jumped-up mandarins, journalists, and socialites of Powertown, as his wife Sondra called Washington. And Gotlieb, for his part, would act as supplicant. That was the reality of asymmetrical diplomacy. Perhaps our brainy, self-confident envoy would be less a "supplicant" than his eleven predecessors. Yet he always knew that being *demandeur* was a byword for the many roles he would play as an ambassador, including "salesman, promoter, public relations operator, huckster, animateur, impresario, and lobbyist." Fundamentally, it was about championing your country's interests and leveraging your influence through building personal relationships, remembering always that Canada is one-tenth the size of the United States.

O'Neill's indifference to him that day was one of Gotlieb's early lessons in humility during his eight feverish years in Washington. There would be many others as he skillfully took his diplomacy beyond the White House and the State Department, where it had traditionally resided. He would record his impressions on the perfervid Washington merry-go-round in his diary in language that was biting, witty, informed, vulnerable, incisive, and frank. Had his unvarnished thoughts come to light then, he would have been pilloried, embarrassed, and recalled. But he was speaking to his diary, and in that less intrusive time, it was a safe haven.

Eventually, in 2006, Gotlieb's private musings were published as *The Washington Diaries 1981–1989*. It is arresting, in today's era of pinchpenny diplomacy, to recall the breadth of relationships that the Gotliebs established as the city's foremost diplomatic couple, largely through their frequent dinners and cocktail parties. They cultivated the players in Ronald Reagan's America: George H.W. Bush, Colin Powell, Bob Strauss, James Baker, Patrick Leahy, and Ed Meese in politics; James Reston, Joe Alsop, Joe Kraft, Art Buchwald, and Ben Bradlee in journalism; Katharine Graham, Evangeline Bruce, Sally Quinn, and the grand tastemakers of Georgetown in society. His diaries are not just a record of whom he met, but how he saw the big bilateral issues of the day: acid rain, cruise-missile testing, lumber, hogs, and, most important, the Canada–United States Free Trade Agreement. They co-mingle with observations on nuclear arms, the Cold War, the Soviet Union, and the Middle East. Gotlieb watches – and chronicles – the debate over the Iran-Contra Scandal, the invasion of Grenada, and the presidential elections of 1984 and 1988.

Oh, what a life it was! Here is his account of September 22, 1983: "Breakfast with Maurice Strong and the very rich and ultra-liberal Congressman Jim Scheuer of New York (he wants us to sue the United States in the World Court over acid rain), a call on Paul Volcker (interest rates), lunch with Larry Eagleburger (the world), then flew to New York at the invitation of Bill Casey . . . to attend a dinner in honour of Sir William Stephenson." Here, all in a day's work, the ambassador confers with a banker (the chair of the Federal Reserve Board), a diplomat (under-secretary of state for Political Affairs), and a spy (the director of the Central Intelligence Agency). He learns nothing about the Middle East from Casey ("a master of obfuscation"), but feels badly later, having attacked Casey personally in a memo to the State Department, when he hears that Casey has cancer. Gotlieb reveals as well that Stephenson, the World War II spymaster, believed Pierre Trudeau was a "communist."

The delightful morsels tumble from the dinner table. Defense Secretary Caspar Weinberger and his wife Jane are the epitome of "a curious snobbism that breeds in Washington." Negotiating for the distribution of Canadian films in the United States with the fabled Jack Valenti is "like negotiating with Stalin." Senator Jennings Randolph of West Virginia is unhinged, Michael Deaver is "an alcoholic," Pamela Harriman is "an international courtesan" (not an original view), George Schultz "may not last" as secretary of state. David Brinkley calls *The Decline of the American Empire*, the Quebecois film Gotlieb screens at the residence, "the worst movie I have ever seen in my life." Gotlieb is incredulous to host a visiting trade delegation of Canadians "crapping all over their government when they are abroad."

All this, and more, find their way into Allan Gotlieb's diary. He scribbled compulsively on planes, trains, and in the backseat of the antique blue-black Oldsmobile that ferried him about town. By the time he quit in 1989, he'd written a half-million words, half of which were published. He had not planned to write for publication, he insists; unlike other well-known diarists, his wasn't a lifelong obsession. In fact, he would not have written a diplomatic diary at all had not Charles Ritchie, the master of the art, advised him on his departure for Washington: "Keep a diary. Above all, you must keep a diary." He did. Years later, on reflection, Gotlieb concluded that "the whole could be seen as greater than its parts, and so, when taken together, a picture might emerge of the enormity, if not the futility, of the task of promoting and defending the interests of Canada in a country which has for so long taken us for granted."

Thirty years after Mr. Gotlieb went to Washington, this is a whole picture. He gives us a sense not only of public diplomacy but practical diplomacy, where advocacy is pointed, entertaining is strategic, and representation matters. In 2011, with events long past and the players long departed or dead, his observations are less likely to offend. Gotlieb published his diary seventeen years after he had left Washington, retired from the public service, and returned to Canada. His musings, however piquant, do not threaten national security. Had they been published in 1986 rather than 2006, though, they would have revealed sensitive matters, such as Canada's negotiating position on free trade or the frailties of personalities whom Gotlieb was courting. Many would have been mortified. Could we imagine the outrage if Arthur Goldberg, the retired Cabinet secretary, ambassador, and high court judge, had opened the *Washington Post* to read that his visitors at Sunday lunch thought he was "a monumental egoist" who sniffed at eating "pasta off paper plates"? Gotlieb, who left Goldberg's table confident that he would no longer lunch with Goldberg on porcelain, paper, or anything else, allowed in his diary that he longed "to be rude." Within its covers, he could be rude, and deliciously so.

That's because the diary is a sanctuary. It's a place to confide and confess, to agonize, insult, and apologize, if only to yourself. It was a way for Gotlieb to unburden himself. It was secret and it would remain secret – at least until its secrets no longer counted. Gotlieb wouldn't put such personal sentiments in his dispatches to Ottawa, if he wrote dispatches; much official business took place on the telephone with the prime minister, the minister of External Affairs, or the undersecretary, or in meetings with them in Ottawa and Washington. When Gotlieb did record secrets, though, he was assured that they would remain secret, the Access to Information Act notwithstanding. Much as he embraced – even pioneered – the practice of public diplomacy, he understood the need for quiet diplomacy, the hallowed tradition of conducting business and airing differences in private. In his day, what happened in Washington stayed in Washington. Today, that's no longer so. Like authority, sin, Christmas, and winter, secrecy isn't what it used to be. Secrecy has lost its sanctity.

In the autumn of 2010, when WikiLeaks began releasing the first of a quarter-million confidential cables to and from American envoys around the world, it was shattering a fundamental assumption of diplomacy. WikiLeaks had stormed the citadel of privacy and carried off its secrets. If, as the *New York Times* said, the record it found was a chronicle of the foreign relations of the United States, it was more a treasure trove of impression, observation, and opinion. The subject of the cables written by American diplomats included Iran's nuclear ambitions, North Korea's future, Guantanamo Bay's detainees, nuclear weapons in Pakistan, and the value of aid to Pakistan. They discussed corruption in Russia and leadership in Georgia. Less weighty, but more salacious, were dispatches on Vladimir Putin's work ethic, Moammar Gadhafi's voluptuous Ukrainian nurse, and the erratic Robert Mugabe. The *Times* published these dispatches under the droll heading "Candid and Frank Assessments." They were. What we read here, though, was not unlike what we read in Allan Gotlieb's diaries – without the wit, erudition, and hauteur of Canada's last Oxonian in Washington.

The difference is that the world was reading the cables when they were still relevant. Making them public could compromise American military and economic interests. No wonder columnist Charles Krauthammer called the work of WikiLeaks "an act of sabotage" against a country at war. When you reveal the names of operatives, the places they worked, their allegiances, and their opinions, and when you let others know your thinking, you do damage. No wonder there was such hostility toward Julian Assange, the fair-haired Australian who acquired the cables from a disgruntled government employee and began showering them on the world's media.

Canada, we should note, was not overlooked in this unprecedented document dump. The diplomats in the U.S. embassy in Ottawa were as busy as the diplomats in other capitals. They dutifully informed Foggy Bottom of the "onslaught" of Canadian television shows, for example, which depicted "nefarious American officials carrying out equally nefarious deeds in Canada, including bombing Quebec and stealing our water." The diplomats shared anxiety over negative images of the United States on Canadian television representing "the insidious popular stereotyping we are increasingly up against in Canada." They noted "the habitual inferiority complex" among Canadians toward the United States, observing our lament over how little attention Americans paid Canada, given the attention we paid them. Not exactly news.

This appears to be the work of an earnest third secretary with a television and too little to do. He (or she) seemed to enjoy monitoring *The Border* and *Little Mosque on the Prairie* and mining them for cultural meaning. Playing television critic was part of writing home about "away," the kind of reportage that diplomats used to do (valuably) when news travelled more slowly and there was no competition from radio, television, and newspapers drawing on their army of foreign correspondents deployed everywhere. In the leaked cables, hinting at the secret archive to come, the American diplomat is realtor, food critic, dance critic, comedian, sociologist, and psychologist. From their perches around the world, they analyze subjects and their countries. In this, no detail is too small. This is the role of the diplomat – or was.

It is also, in truth, what Gotlieb was doing in his diary. What diplomats recorded in their dispatches for the State Department, Gotlieb did in his diary. His reader, in the 1980s, was himself. Their readers were their colleagues at headquarters. All were thought to be trustworthy, but Gotlieb's damning diary remained confidential; their damning dispatches did not. This is the critical difference between then and now.

So what impact will WikiLeaks have on the practice of diplomacy? What does it mean for the security of sources and the expression of ideas and intentions? In a word, it declares that nothing is secure anymore. If, in the world's wealthiest country, with the world's biggest defence and intelligence establishment, a malcontent can crack the system, copy its contents, and drop cables like leaflets over occupied Europe, nothing is safe. And while we can change the locks and reconfigure the codes, it is unlikely to restore confidence in the way diplomats communicate and go about their work. Nationals are now less likely to talk to diplomats, let alone cooperate with them, particularly in war zones or in repressive regimes, if they cannot be assured their dealings are confidential. Blowing their cover could endanger lives, their own and others'.

On a practical level, diplomats will be more careful with what they write if they think it could be leaked to the public. They will commit nothing to paper. The advantage here is that all those desk officers in Ottawa, Washington, London, Paris, and beyond will have fewer dispatches to read from their counterparts in the field. The disadvantage is that what they do read will be so empty and so bland that it will not be worth reading at all. The loss will be to historians, as well, who are still coping with the decline of letter writing in the era of electronic mail; it is the difference between communication and correspondence. Terrified of seeing their words in print, diplomats will deprive posterity of their honest observations. When the files are released, as they will be eventually, we will be none the wiser. It won't be worth the wait.

The end of secrecy will diminish the currency of diplomacy. Certainly reportage, which was already becoming a blunt arrow in the diplomatic quiver, will add little value to the making of foreign policy. Before WikiLeaks, secrecy was already under strain in a society embracing transparency in state craft. This is an age of openness, in which there are no secrets; today de Tocqueville would be *Tattler*. The advance of technology and its prying eyes and ears have brought light into places it dared not go before. We are not only in the bedrooms of the state; we are in its staterooms, too. The cheapest mobile telephone has a camera and an audio recorder, allowing us to capture word and image and transmit them anywhere fully and instantaneously. Anything can now show up on Facebook, where people feel inclined to put their lives on display, or on Twitter, where they announce every detail of their lives, no matter how trivial, mundane, or inane. They post their musings on personal blogs or comment on other sites, unedited and unfiltered, even if their views are racist, prejudiced, or just dumb.

This is a sharing society. First access was a virtue, then a verb. It isn't that everyone will get fifteen minutes of fame anymore, as Andy Warhol famously predicted; now everyone may well get a lifetime, even an eternity, with the right technology. And as much as it may confer fame, it may also inflict infamy.

The public square is the new confessional. For every sin there is now a priest. Your absolution is attention, as if that were enough. It's a sea change in attitude. It is incomprehensible to the post-war generation that did not talk about the battles they fought, the Holocaust they survived, and the Depression they suffered. Now we talk about anything. Discretion? Restraint? Prudence? They're passé. Today we talk, talk, talk.

For the diplomatic diarist, like Allan Gotlieb, this means everything. The more we crave candour in diplomacy, natural voyeurs that we are, the more valuable we make the diary. The water-marked, leather-bound, well-thumbed, hand-written diary of unintelligible jottings from groggy early mornings and sodden late nights is something rare today (as is any diary, regardless of the form or context). Rest assured, WikiLeaks will give this old art new life. For those in authority who absolutely must record what happens to them because life cannot pass by unnoticed, the diary will become the last refuge. For those who cherish the witty and worthy observations of the likes of Charles Ritchie, Harold Nicholson, and Isaiah Berlin, among others, it is the only place left, the last dominion of confidentiality. Much like the live stage performance has enhanced the entertainer's value in a culture of free downloads and pirated songs, the uniqueness of the diary will become sharply apparent in a culture swimming in superficiality, immediacy, and transparency. None is the particular virtue of the diary, which takes the long view of things. It is deeper, denser, and, above all, discreet.

As Allan Gotlieb shows us, a diary can have humour, tartness, and, Lord knows, gossip. It may well be light and frivolous. It may also be trenchant and illuminating. Hell, it may even disclose what everybody knows, as Leonard Cohen says. But a diary still has what almost nothing else has today: the *authority* of secrecy. And in diplomacy, as in history, that matters.

There was a time when personal journals came with lock and key. For WikiLeaks, those purveyors of purloined information bent on destroying the zone of privacy, these would be no deterrent. But in another time, the journal with the lock clasped said: *This is not for your eyes. Stay away. Respect my privacy.* In a society where freedom of information is a right, it respectfully dissents. Your right to know my secrets, it warns, ends where my words begin.

Alas, these are not questions that Ambassador Gotlieb had to ponder when he was blackening pages during his glorious, sun-drenched season in Washington a generation ago. He was unafraid to write what he felt in his diary, assured that it would remain secret as long as he was there. If it didn't, he also knew that it would be his undoing. At the same time, he knew that the era of quiet diplomacy, at least between Canada and the United States, was yielding to public diplomacy, which would, by its very nature, have to take place in the garish light of day. And that's what has happened.

There are reasons to fear that we won't see diplomatic diaries anymore. There is less time, less inclination to write, and less ability to write. Actually, though, there are now more reasons to think that we will hear more, much more, of satraps and supplicants. History and literature will be the beneficiaries. For this we can thank WikiLeaks.

THE NEW "NEW" DIPLOMACY:
Open Diplomacy and Open Policy Development

Arif Lalani

Now you're still going to need smart people in this world.
But part of the job for your smart people in this world is
to identify, recognize, and then connect to the other
smart people that are out there.[1]

HENRY CHESBROUGH

To be an effective ambassador in the United States it is
necessary to rip up the old rules of diplomacy and follow
new ones which, however, are ill defined, uncharted,
treacherous, and capable of leading the foreign representative into troubled waters.[2]

ALLAN GOTLIEB

Like his mentor, Marcel Cadieux, under-secretary in the
1960s and ambassador to Washington in the 1970s, Allan
Gotlieb believed in networks. He headed to Washington in
the fall of 1981 confident that he would soon build the traditional network of White House aides and State Department
bureaucrats needed to advance Canada's interests and understand U.S. politics in a way that contributed to sound policy
decisions in Ottawa. How this was done in post-Watergate
Washington, where power and influence were shifting about,
surprised him. It delighted him too, and the ambassador and

his wife, Sondra, were quickly engulfed in a very public, kalei-
doscopic network of congressmen and senators, bureaucrats
and powerbrokers, celebrities and socialites. The new diplomacy, Gotlieb told us enthusiastically, then and later, was
"public diplomacy."[3]

When I headed for Kabul in 2007, I carried Gotlieb's
account of his American adventures, *The Washington Diaries,*
with me, prepared to be charmed, amused, and educated. And
I was. But over the next few years in Afghanistan, and later at
business school in London, I encountered an important truth:
today's networks are vastly different from the ones Gotlieb
encountered in Ronald Reagan's Washington. Globalization,
new technologies and social media, and the explosion of non-
traditional players have created vast networks, where everyone,
not just the most accomplished or the most forceful personality, has a shot at influencing world affairs. Where Gotlieb
might have crammed eight or twelve or fourteen meetings into
a busy day, with today's social media, his successor will engage
a larger, more diverse network, 24/7. Open diplomacy and
open policy development – building vast global networks to
harness ideas and nurture support everywhere, all the time –
are the hallmarks of modern diplomacy.

Diplomacy in context

Many of the challenges that confront the contemporary foreign and trade ministry and its occupants are hardly new. As
Drew Fagan's contribution to this collection points out, the
broad changes observed in the 1970s – the ballooning policy
agenda, the proliferation of regional and global institutions,

and the increasing relevance of domestic and non-state actors – haunt us still. Indeed, in many cases they have grown more complex as globalization has accelerated. Provincial, regional, and municipal governments, as well as the private sector and a host of nongovernmental organizations routinely demand to be heard in discussions on Canada's foreign and trade policy. Almost every federal government department has its bureau of international affairs, and the blurring of official and personal views, created by the new forms of informal communication, makes it tougher than ever to craft coherent and effective policy.

At the same time, globalization is creating a different, more powerful, and more interconnected citizenry, with demands and expectations about how Canada will conduct itself in the world. These Canadians travel, work, and live abroad in ever-increasing numbers. According to the Asia Pacific Foundation, Canada, with as many as 2.8 million Canadians (or 8 per cent of its population) resident abroad, has one of the world's highest proportions of nationals living outside its borders.[4] At home, Canada's demographic landscape is changing too: in 2006, the proportion of Canadians born outside the country reached its largest level in seventy-five years,[5] and in 2008, the country set a new record by admitting 520,000 immigrants.[6]

These kinds of numbers bring their own challenges. Diaspora groups can be vocal and active. The Israel-Lebanon crisis in the summer of 2006 and the Tamil drummers who brought both downtown Toronto and Ottawa to a standstill in April 2009 illustrate how closely national and international issues are intertwined. This is often good news, a lesson driven home in Kabul, where the embassy I headed in 2007–08 worked hard to help establish a network of Canadians in

Afghanistan (a kinder, gentler CIA). My compatriots made terrific local partners. Helping bright young Canadians from a variety of backgrounds to "self-organize" and collaborate with the embassy on shared reconstruction and development objectives made a great deal of sense for everyone involved. Embassy staff, in particular, welcomed the chance to harness these "outside" perspectives. That experience, which underlined the value of the diplomat's network, left me wondering how and where else these global citizens might be mobilized and their expertise acknowledged.

Technology too is changing our diplomacy. When I joined External Affairs (as the department was still called in 1991), we filled in chits for overseas telephone calls and we walked urgent telegrams down several floors to our "communicators" for transmission to posts. And then, we waited. Today, there's little waiting. Consultations that used to take a week now take fifteen minutes. Putting together a PowerPoint presentation in Afghanistan for the prime minister or Cabinet might involve contributions from fifty bureaucrats in a dozen different agencies operating on several continents. And it will all be done within twenty-four hours. As Chilean diplomat-scholar Jorge Heine recently put it, for diplomacy, as for so much else, technological change means "the compression of time and space."[7]

The same high-tech changes have empowered individual citizens, who are able to learn, organize, and express themselves in unprecedented ways, both at home and abroad. The Canadian Chamber of Commerce in Hong Kong, for instance, has more than 1,200 members and is one of the largest and most influential business networks in the Asia-Pacific region. And these individuals no longer represent just "public opinion." They deliver policy outputs by engaging in the whole range of transnational activity that "exists above the state, below the state, and through the state."[8] Few, if any, emerging international issues or opportunities can be dealt with by government alone. Partnering with those outside the government is becoming crucial in order to deliver meaningful results. Countries that understand this and position themselves to adopt a "whole-of-nation" approach to advancing their interests stand to grow their relative influence. That this change is already underway in Washington was apparent in Secretary of State Hillary Clinton's sweeping review of American diplomacy last fall. The United States, she insisted, can, and must, "leverage civilian power by connecting businesses, philanthropists, and citizens' groups with partner governments to perform tasks governments alone cannot."[9]

Open diplomacy requires open policy development

Governments must adjust their diplomacy to respond to these global demographic and technological phenomena. Diplomacy must become faster, more transparent, and interactive, changes that one observer has described as moving from "club diplomacy" to "network diplomacy."[10] Foreign ministries must understand and engage with their citizens across the globe to improve policies and programmes, enhance their influence, and remain accountable. Today's global challenges and opportunities require foreign ministries to adopt a new type of diplomacy that is more open than ever before to outside voices. The issues, actors, and technologies both compel and enable contemporary diplomats to network differently.

One vital way that the Department of Foreign Affairs and

International Trade (DFAIT) can work better to equip its diplomats and policy makers to operate in their networked environment, taking advantage of the growing connections between actors in global affairs, is by embracing an idea that I dub "open policy development." The concept, rooted in private sector developments, is not hard to grasp. Historically, private industry (like government) relied almost entirely on its own resources. In-house research and development operations imagined services and products, which were then thrown onto market. Knowledge was power, and jealously guarded.

That's changed. Over the past two decades, the private sector has increasingly relied on Open Innovation, an idea that embraces the capacity of Internet-based technologies and social media to build extensive networks and exchange vast amounts of information in multiple directions. By increasing the permeability of business and reaching out to consumers, partners, and even competitors to trade ideas and solutions and pool their knowledge, small firms and multinational corporations alike have shown that they can develop better products faster and more cheaply.[11] Procter and Gamble, the multinational manufacturer of consumers' goods, for instance, derives almost half its new products from ideas developed with outside collaborators. IBM, Google, Starbucks, and even Ottawa's own Lee Valley Tools have employed the concept to generate products using the ideas of their consumers and users.

Our product is information and knowledge, digested and transformed into policy advice. Open policy development imports the principles of open innovation to government, exploring how DFAIT might begin to see the crowd of voices outside its doorstep as potential allies rather than competitors. Open policy development employs social media, or Web

2.0 tools, to engage policy stakeholders in fresh ways, with a view to leveraging a range of external perspectives early in the policy development process. In developing foreign policy, we recognize that Canada's diplomats and public servants must integrate ideas from the outside while maintaining a credible critical mass of internal policy capacity to absorb original ideas.

Adopting this fresh policy-making paradigm will help assure our external partners and clients that diplomats and public servants do not have a monopoly on good ideas. Traditionally, policies were crafted inside the department with stakeholders consulted at specific points along the process and only when options were sufficiently ready (some might say "cooked") for outside eyes. But open diplomacy and open policy development both insist that foreign-policy-makers connect with traditional and non-traditional actors, forming confident and trusting relationships with them in a way that allows for collaboration throughout the policy development process.

This approach is untried and difficult. There are federal, legal, and regulatory requirements around bilingualism, privacy, and information management that still must be overcome. More important, there are cultural barriers in our workplace – in overseas missions, in the Canadian cities, and at "Fort Pearson" – that will get in the way. This was evident at a DFAIT "policy jam" that the policy planning bureau organized in November 2010. During our regular leadership conference, we connected over three hundred executive-level officers from around the world in a virtual network and invited them all, regardless of their expertise, to join policy discussions on three broad themes: global governance, the foreign and trade ministry of the future, and global citizens.

The process forced "experts" to apply their craft on unfamiliar terrain, and left many uncomfortable. Deputy ministers were more impressed. They were especially intrigued by the broad range of ideas that surfaced in our conversations around global citizens.

Social media and the networks they spawn are sprawling, messy things, and they threaten to rearrange the comfortable hierarchical distinctions we value too much. They also undermine our control of the policy making process. Our old networks were tame and shuttered affairs, closed both by conviction and the practical difficulties of bringing large numbers of trusted collaborators to the table. This is no longer the case, and consultative networks can quickly take on a life of their own, leaving policy makers scrambling to catch up. Despite these challenges, open policy development holds great promise as a transformative paradigm for the way we make policy and do diplomacy. Imagining the shape of things to come, three key ideas should animate our efforts: diversity, collaboration, and openness.

Diversity

The open policy development model embraces networks as multipliers of diverse and different viewpoints, which are especially good at forging linkages between large numbers of apparently unrelated and unconnected interlocutors. As they do now, policy makers must continue to seek out obvious stakeholders in DFAIT, other government departments, and the broader community with ideas and expertise to contribute. There are already good examples where the department has used social media platforms to mobilize these traditional networks in new ways. During Canada's term as G-8 and G-20 chair, for instance, the summit management team created a virtual platform for sherpas and policy makers from other governments to share information. Similarly, DFAIT's Stabilization and Reconstruction Task Force (START), which coordinates Canada's engagements in such fragile states as Afghanistan, Haiti, and Sudan, is a founding partner in the International Stabilization and Peacebuilding Initiative (ISPI). An informal, working-level network of governments as well as domestic and international NGOs, ISPI collaborates through a secure Internet site on shared efforts to enhance civilian peace-building capacity.

But we can do more. Virtual networks are inexpensive, and access is cheap, allowing us to expand those networks beyond our usual comfort range to bring unconventional perspectives to bear. In earlier models – dumb collaboration – policy-makers typically invited outside experts to comment on their polished ideas and programs. The new model – smart collaboration – places a premium on identifying problems and interests, and using social media's huge potential for finding new partners to develop novel solutions. Confronted with the challenge of delivering the H1N1 vaccination to masses of Canadians, for instance, health officials in Quebec turned to Disney for inspiration for handling crowd control.[12] Similarly, it might make more sense for DFAIT to consult a young computer coder with an interest in global affairs and an ability to speak the language of Middle East protesters than the regular suspects from the Munk School or the Centre for International Governance Innovation (CIGI). Or, why not invite Bay Street bankers and fund managers to join the regular roster of NGOs and bureaucrats shaping Canadian aid policy? There is no monopoly on good ideas, assessments, or solutions – within divisions, bureaus, or departments. Good ideas are out there, and we need to build open networks to help us find them.

Collaboration

Opening up the policy-development process will not be easy. Genuine collaboration does not come readily to the classically-trained diplomat. During DFAIT's human rights policy consultations that I observed over a decade ago, officials typically headed into the room determined to surrender as little ground as possible, while the assembled NGOs were just as resolute in rejecting our views. It was a happy dialogue of the deaf that allowed each side to check off their respective boxes, labelled "consultations."

Networks generate a different kind of consultation. Rather than one-off conferences, they encourage long-term collaborative conversations, where ideas can be shared, assessed, and critiqued in more careful and reflective ways. The leisure to reflect on his experiences, Cadieux shrewdly remarked long ago in his primer for young diplomats, was an essential prerequisite for sound policy making.[13]

Collaboration that goes beyond the usual suspects and forums will rarely be neat or tidy. When outside voices, sometimes raised and strident, reject our views, they must be engaged rather than dismissed. The outcomes will be less predictable – a risky business for policy makers. These kinds of conversations will clearly take more time and energy than perhaps we might like. Even so, they represent the essential building blocks for sustained and trusting relationships.

Openness

Open diplomacy and open policy development are collaborative exercises, and thus invite, or even force, policy makers to take bold and intelligent risks when sharing information. Reflecting its technological origins, the open policy development model starts by acknowledging that information seeks to be free, and assumes that information should therefore be shared as widely as possible. To craft better policy, we must let others use our knowledge and build on our ideas, and develop their own contributions to Canada's foreign and trade policy agenda. With a little common sense, a handful of accepted practices like the Chatham House Rule, and a willingness to trust our networks, we can build safe and secure online communities for smart information sharing. Indeed, to craft policy on Iran and the Middle East, DFAIT's planning staff have recently created an "emerging issues network" that embraces government officials and scholars from Canada, the Middle East, Europe, Asia, and the United States. The network includes aerospace and high-tech professionals, researchers from the C.D. Howe Institute and the Agha Khan Foundation, and businessmen from the Canadian Council of Chief Executives. The conversations have brought outside parties into the policy-making process at an earlier stage than is usual or comfortable. But the results have been worth it.

All this may sound a little odd in the wake of WikiLeaks. But the lessons are paradoxical. In today's transparent and interconnected world, I believe that we need to be more open on more things, while better safeguarding a smaller number of important items.

Conclusion

We live in what I would call an integrated, extroverted, overnight world. Complex challenges require integrated approaches. A world where more and more is in the open – where extroverts seem to have the day, where assessment and opinion is required almost overnight, where organizations have to function 24/7 across geography and culture – requires a new approach to my profession too.

Open diplomacy and open policy development will demand a difficult change in our policy-making culture. Like business and civil society, government and foreign ministries must move, and move quickly, from a closed and hierarchical system to a faster, more open, and interactive environment. Open diplomacy implies that others outside the organization are essential to our product development and its marketing, and to creating and implementing policy. This change will not come easily and it does not sit well with everyone, just as Ambassador Gotlieb's very public diplomacy unsettled some at the time. His approach subsequently became a model for the rest of us.

We should be clear though that this model – of leveraging the creativity of others – does not absolve us of our ultimate responsibility. Virtual networks, like the glittering network that once gathered around the Gotliebs, ultimately aim at generating better and sounder policy decisions and recommendations. In the final analysis, we remain responsible for harvesting from these networks, from the facts and information so easily available to those who wish to look for it. We are responsible for a view and perspective that is still ours to stand behind and for. It is we who have to make sense of a confusing world for a frantic minister or busy prime minister. While more people can help us interpret this world, the final accountability remains with the person giving the advice. That hasn't changed since Gotlieb's time.

*The views expressed in this chapter are the author's alone and do not represent the views of the Government of Canada or the Department of Foreign Affairs and International Trade. The author would like to thank Niall Cronin and Greg Donaghy for their essential work on this draft; and Mary Halloran for helpful comments on an earlier draft.

Notes

1 Henry Chesbrough, "Open Innovation and Open Business Models: A New Approach to Industrial Innovation," 2008, video broadcast, 10:48, presentation to Open Innovation Speaker Series, http://www.youtube.com/watch?v=lQdb9LmXK-I.

2 Allan Gotlieb, *"I'll Be with You in a Minute, Mr. Ambassador": The Education of a Canadian Diplomat in Washington* (Toronto: University of Toronto Press, 1991), 44.

3 Ibid., vii.

4 Don DeVoretz, "Canada's Secret Province: 2.8 Million Canadians Abroad," *Working Paper Series, Special Issue* 9 no. 5 (October 2009).

5 "Census Snapshot – Immigration in Canada: A Portrait of the Foreign-born Population, 2006 Census," Statistics Canada, March 28, 2011, http://www.statcan.gc.ca/pub/11-008-x/2008001/article/10556-eng.htm#1.

6 "Speaking notes for the Honourable Jason Kenney, P.C., M.P., Minister of Citizenship, Immigration and Multiculturalism, at the Eleventh National Metropolis Conference," Citizenship and Immigration Canada, March 20, 2009, accessed March 28, 2011, http://www.cic.gc.ca/english/department/media/speeches/2009/2009–03–20.asp.

7 Jorge Heine, introductory remarks at a panel discussion on modern diplomacy, International Development Research Centre, March 15, 2011.

8 Anne-Marie Slaughter, "America's Edge: Power in the Networked Century," *Foreign Affairs* 88 no. 1 (January/February 2009): 94.

9 Hillary Rodham Clinton, "Leading Through Civilian Power: Redefining American Diplomacy and Development," *Foreign Affairs* 89 no. 6 (November/December 2010): 17.

10 Jorge Heine, introductory remarks, March 15, 2011.

11 Henry Chesbrough, *Open Innovation: The New Imperative for Creating and Profiting from Technology* (Boston: Harvard Business School Press, 2003).

12   Ingrid Peritz, "Quebec's Disney-inspired Solution to Flu-shot Crisis," *Globe and Mail*, November 15, 2009.

13   Marcel Cadieux, *The Canadian Diplomat: An Essay in Definition* (Toronto: University of Toronto Press, 1963), 33.

conclusion
looking forward

DIGITAL DIPLOMACY

William Thorsell

Diplomacy 101

I came to diplomacy early and superficially. Fresh from the University of Alberta at the age of twenty-one, I was made manager of the Western Canada Pavilion at Expo 67, and thus the ranking "diplomat" for the four western provinces in Montreal during the heady year of Canada's Centennial.

Suddenly, I was on lists for luncheons in the Pavillon d'Honneur attended by white-gloved waiters behind every chair. I was at the opening ceremonies for countless events and national days, at cocktail parties with myriad hosts under setting suns over the St. Lawrence River, guide to the Queen and other theatrical visits to our pavilion, in excellent seats at the Expo Theatre for opera and dance – in sum, I participated fully in the froth of diplomacy in the world of display, consumption, pretence, and celebration that was Expo 67.

It gave me an appetite for more.

Our hosting of Expo 67 gave Canada the protocol priority at Expo 70 in Japan, having hosted the previous World Exposition in Montreal, and I nabbed the job of protocol officer for Canada. As the number-one protocol stop for the entire site, and with the biggest and flashiest pavilion – a mirrored pyramid designed by Massey-Erickson – we were at the centre of the diplomatic action.

The Emperor of Japan would tour Canada's pavilion as his single symbolic visit to all participating countries. The preparations for this tour consumed months of my time, in conjunction with the Imperial Household, and taught me much about the importance of unimportant things.

We established a ranking system for VIP visits, with the lowest (five) meriting only free access to the pavilion's exhibits through a VIP tunnel, and the highest (one) producing an honour guard of Mounties on steeds, a lavish dinner, and an Inuit carving. Each morning's planning meeting saw a brutal separation of prospective visitors into castes. It was guilty fun.

But Japan went beyond the social diversions of Montreal: this was Canada after all, and Canada abroad. I learned more about the heft of diplomacy in subsequent months. Canada had just re-established diplomatic relations with Gabon after its treatment of Quebec as an "independent nation" at an international conference in the early 1960s. On Gabon's national day at Expo 70, Gabon's representative should have visited Canada on his way to any other pavilion.

Instead, Gabon's brilliantly robed pooh-bah visited the Quebec pavilion first – for forty-five minutes – before his three-minute stride across the plaza of Canada itself. (Quebec, Ontario, and British Columbia had their own pavilions at Expo 70, adding to both the gravitas and the incoherence of Canada's presence.)

This deliberate slight required action.

Our commissioner general, Patrick Reid, called a crisis meeting in his office. Canada's honour was at stake and retaliation was essential. Mr. Reid was scheduled to attend a reception for his fellow ambassadors given by Gabon later that day. In a brilliant, stiletto manoeuvre, he decided I should be sent in his stead as a human diplomatic insult.

As the lowly protocol officer, I was instructed to arrive late and flagrantly at the reception, announce myself as Canada's representative, eschew a libation, and leave post-haste. Happily it was raining, so I was slightly sodden, adding to the offensive aspect. Everything went to plan, and with a haughty mien I came, I saw, and I re-conquered.

Trays of gin awaited at the Canadian pavilion, where I returned with gleeful tales of shocked faces and grisly rumblings. We celebrated into the night, unaware that the next "crisis" would involve our own prime minister, Pierre Trudeau, up against the Most Excellent, starchy Ambassador of Japan itself. That diplomatic debacle would end at a draw in a discotheque in the mid-morning hours. (The Marlon Brando incident was another matter.)

Diplomacy operates at many levels, and sometimes has to do with significant things, such as security, trade, human rights, and the environment. The quotidian practice of diplomacy, however, can validate its reputation as the codification of foible and the validation of pride. These Molière-esque aspects of the craft are not much affected by the deep tides of change that can profoundly alter the diplomatic game when the stakes are high.

The context in which diplomats ply their craft has changed enormously in the last century. The field of diplomacy has grown to include many more influential players, and the pace, risks, and rewards have altered to require new skill sets and intuitions. We cannot know precisely how diplomacy will morph in light of the digital revolution, but we can observe some outlines. And we can see where, one hundred years ago, a different river was crossed.

The decline of Cabinet diplomacy

The First World War was an inflection point in the history of diplomacy. New species of public opinion and radical ideologies broadened and nullified the diplomatic field respectively. The gentlemen's club defined by the Congress of Vienna a century earlier would never be the same, whatever its achievements and pretentions.

The French writer Romain Rolland was vacationing in Switzerland on August 4, 1914, as Europe plunged into a seventy-five-year conflict that would conclude with the fall of the Berlin Wall in 1989. The most sophisticated civilization on Earth was headed to criminal self-destruction at a scale unprecedented since humans discovered the tool, the weapon, and the power of small distinctions to wreak great havoc.

Rolland quickly identified the familiar culprit in this incipient tragedy: diplomacy – "Cabinet diplomacy" – was a game of elite accommodation, and the elites had failed unforgivably to avoid disaster. He said this war was a product of the "controlling classes, governments, financial oligarchies, churches and the supposed intellectual elite – who have led the people to this inept killing." The people themselves were largely irrelevant to the course of events, *comme d'habitude*.

History was typically directed by a governing class, in this case a morbidly corrupt class soaked in the cynicism of the *fin de siècle*. In this analysis, Rolland expressed the paradigm of a dying age. His view was anachronistic: in practice, the elites were losing their grip.

Across the channel, Bertrand Russell had a different explanation for the bloody appetites he saw that night in Trafalgar Square, where "the anticipation of carnage was delightful to something like 90 per cent of the population." Yes, he cited the "set of official gentlemen, living luxurious lives, mostly stupid," who had presided over the descent into madness, but Russell perceived the popular hunger itself for war as a new and almost irresistible force: "Those who saw the London crowds during the nights leading up to the declaration of war saw a whole population, hitherto peaceable and humane, precipitated in a few days down the steep slope to primitive barbarism, letting loose in a moment the instincts of hatred and blood lust against which the whole fabric of society has been raised."

What could diplomacy do with its arcane designs against the novel forces of industrial capitalism that, in Russell's view, fomented such appetites for rapacious adventure in so many, for such meager rational gains? If once diplomacy had claimed to determine relations among states, now popular will, transformed by a revolution of means, was also a driving force in history. Diplomacy was confronted by an array of new material forces that had led to "total war."

(In his memoir, Christopher Hitchens writes, of Ian McEwan, that "his novels are almost always patrolling some difficult frontier between the speculative and the unseen and the ways in which material reality reimposes itself." Such was the dynamic facing diplomacy in the early twentieth century, argued Russell – a new "material reality" was refashioning diplomacy itself.)

In Vienna, Sigmund Freud shared the enthusiasm for war, exclaiming in his own anti-Semitic Hapsburg capital that "for the first time in thirty years I feel myself to be an Austrian and feel like giving this not very hopeful Empire another chance." Such was the power of "mass psychology" in 1914, affecting the father of psychoanalysis himself.

In every country, poets and scientists, artists and philosophers have rushed to escape the *fin de siècle*'s ennui by enlisting at the front, confirming that diplomacy had somehow become an adjunct to new mass phenomena.

Whether due to an emotionally stultifying industrial regime, as Russell believed, or to what Freud soon described as a "lust for killing" that had been over-repressed by Victorian morality, public opinion would now play a role in the relations among states not before seen. (Incidentally, Russell gave voice to the unusual phenomenon of public pacifism in the First World War, and spent some time in jail for it.)

Paul Kennedy observes in *The Rise and Fall of the Great Powers*:

> The Old World statesmen and foreign offices had always found it difficult either to understand or deal with economic issues; but perhaps an even more disruptive feature, to those fondly looking back at the cabinet diplomacy of the nineteenth century, was the increasing influence of mass public opinion upon international affairs during the 1920s and 1930s. . . . But the problem with "public opinion" after 1919 was that many sections of it did not match that fond Gladstonian and Wilsonian vision of a liberal, educated, fair-minded populace,

imbued with internationalist ideas, utilitarian assumptions, and respect for the rule of law.

So it was not just the fact, but the nature of public opinion that would reshape the world. Woodrow Wilson's commitment to "self-determination" of peoples in 1918 clearly acknowledged a new locus of power in public sentiment. But radical ideologies would go further, and challenge not only the claim of elites to structure relations among states, but assumptions about the very purpose of those relations. The forcible export of psychotic revolution became the goal in Germany, the Soviet Union, and beyond, and messianic revolution was not an export for which the coin of diplomacy had much purchase.

The wrinkles in Neville Chamberlain's piece of paper at Munich in 1938 spoke eloquently enough: material forces – technological, psychological, and ideological – expressed through mass movements, drove the historical drama now. If Munich was a "triumph of diplomacy," diplomacy was a cuckold in a world of deadly serious men.

After 1945, with diplomacy apparently resurrected at the United Nations, public opinion waxed and waned in its effect on foreign policy, but mattered much when much mattered. This was most apparent during the Vietnam War where, in the United States and beyond, "Cabinet diplomacy" found itself visibly beleaguered again. The rise of television generated the first "living room war," and "that's the way it is" confirmed public opinion as a decisive force in the determination of policy in critical times.

Opposition to nuclear armament in the 1970s, global epidemics, poverty, and environmentalism in the 1980s, required governments to respond to well-organized mass movements as never before; television again created pan-national constituencies for issues that transcended traditional national interests.

In Canada, negotiation of the Free Trade Agreement (FTA) with the United States in the 1980s saw the creation of unprecedented formal advisory groups representing economic and social sectors as part of the diplomatic "team." The arresting image from the debate over the FTA was that of an eraser eliminating the Canadian-American border in a Liberal party television ad – and a pencil restoring it in a Conservative rejoinder. What voter was not a "diplomat" in that theatrical media event?

But television itself was about to be eclipsed by something of a qualitatively different nature.

Seeking a theory of change

The Holy Grail for students of history has been something called "a theory of change." We can document massive shifts in social and political landscapes over time, but cannot easily explain them even in retrospect by a meaningful theory of change. (Certainty that they are the results of acts by the "great men of history" does not suffice.) Where does change come from? What causes and shapes the great revolutions of humanity over time?

Marx made a remarkable effort at such a theory in his identification of the "relationship to the means of production" – as either an owner or employee seeking advantage in economic work. Dialectical materialism offered an impressive theory of change that converted (and ultimately oppressed and murdered) millions before it fell of its own weight in the 1980s.

Bertrand Russell explored the same nexus, but focused on its psychological rather than material effects. Russell plumbed the worker's personal, alienating "experience" of the industrial system, rather than his "interest" in its spoils. (Ironically, fascists would mine this insight into the collective "id" most effectively.)

Russell and Marx recognized that technology had fundamentally altered social relationships and had given public "opinion" a newly discrete, powerful role in human affairs. In retrospect, their interpretations were over-specific and arrogantly prescriptive, but their insights into the springs of change were prescient.

It seems well arguable now that technological innovation above all else alters economic and social relations among states. Paul Kennedy illuminated this well, and focused on shifting advantages in technology as a motor of global affairs. States rise and ebb due to the "technological and organizational breakthroughs which bring a greater advantage to one society than to another."

The Industrial Revolution created the urban agglomerations, literacy, and media that raised living standards, expanded military establishments, and created effective public opinion. One of the casualties of this new technological order was "Cabinet diplomacy," as we have seen, and have witnessed repeatedly since 1919.

The question now is how the management of international affairs will be affected by our current dominant technology – the precocious technology of the "digital age."

It can be said that the printing press allowed one person to speak to many, that the telephone allowed one to speak to one, and that the Internet now allows many to speak to many.

(Radio, cinema, and television are equivalent to the printing press, though relatively "cooler" – television – or "hotter" – print media – in Marshall McLuhan's language.)

Each of these media fashioned a landscape of power. It was often said in the age of newspapers that you did not want to get into an argument with a man who bought printer's ink by the railcar load. True, the printing press allowed for more diversity and dissemination of ideas, but in practice, economic barriers to entry gave unparalleled influence to the "press barons" and their editors in framing public opinion, and thus political reality.

The telephone permitted one-on-one communication, and so also abetted diversity in opinion and organization – but this too was in the context of powerful gatekeepers in the mass media. The "cabinet" in Cabinet diplomacy now included the owners of centralized communication technology as proxies for the public, joined by a widening group of academics and interest groups with access to major organs of news and opinion.

The rituals of diplomacy would endure – the discreet, promiscuous couplings of diplomats in short-term postings, with their premiums on gossip, gamesmanship, hypocrisy, and a tolerance for booze. But responsibility for the big issues rose higher in the political hierarchy as public opinion weighed more heavily on the conduct of foreign affairs, and thus on the politics of domestic affairs. Career diplomats in their important posts were often left in the wake.

If this was the consequence in good part of centralized communication technology, what would its reverse entail – the distribution of the "printing press" and broadcast licence to millions of individuals, suddenly capable of reaching millions more?

What happens when a hotline (such as was famously installed between the White House and the Kremlin after the Cuban missile crisis) is supplanted by online – two voices joined by millions? When many can talk to many in real time, when information can be disseminated in great volume instantly, when "authority" is no longer attached to metastasizing news and opinion, how does the practice of diplomacy change again?

The conditions of the digital age

The fundamental factor in understanding technology as an agent of change is its consequence for the distribution of power. One condition of power is control of information, a fact appreciated by pharaohs and witch doctors, professors, entrepreneurs, journalists, scientists, and popes across the ages. Thus we see censorship in every polity in every age, with the greatest control exercised by those with the strongest convictions and weakest arguments.

It is now the individual's relationship to the means of "information" – rather than to the means of "production" – that most shapes the contemporary world. Information is not ultimately the opiate of the masses, as was proffered during the early stage of network television; it is the empowerment of the masses – for better and worse.

We are aware of this "abraxas" quality in the Internet age – the almost perfect match between good and evil in the potential of any new technology.

The formula $E = mc^2$ created both the capacity for human self-destruction and liberation from many constraints. So it was with the printing press, with the telephone, radio, television, and now the Internet: each changed the landscape of power with no "opinion" on how that power would be employed.

So the Internet becomes the finest library in the history of humanity, available to more people at less cost than anything imaginable only twenty years ago, but also an infinite source of inconsequential diversion.

So the Internet becomes the best vehicle for the dissemination of hatred and potential crimes against humanity since the printing press and the availability of gunpowder – but also a tool for social justice in a radically decentralized information system.

Cabinet diplomacy flourished in an era when control of information was almost personal in its nature, and so the context for those who directed it was small.

Diplomacy in the age of mass communication was shaped by "the crowd" – grounded in industrial systems and mass communications, manipulated by dictators and ideologues, massaged and regurgitated by "press barons" and parasitic interest groups.

The common factor in these ages was management of information from a centre – a dramatically widening centre to be sure – but a centre nonetheless.

What happens when the centre does not hold? This is the question of our age.

The arena of diplomacy in the digital age

The diplomatic pouch has been torn asunder by the digital age, which is characterized by immediacy, transparency, profligacy, and universality.

- Immediacy means that the interval between events and a required response to those events is now very short indeed.
- Transparency means that control of information about interests, strategies, strengths, and weaknesses is substantially diluted, both among national players and between them and many publics. Critical information is widely shared, leaked, or intuited, and thus is power. Diplomacy is practised live in a public arena with spectators in the billions.
- Profligacy means that many more players now influence relations among states – more quickly and conspicuously. A multilateral system has become a multidimensional one, vastly multiplying the options and contingencies in play.
- Universality means that the issues requiring diplomatic attention are enormously broader in their reference – far beyond traditional boundaries of the "national interest." The national interest has become a calculation made in a global context, which transcends familiar economic and security concerns.

These characteristics, grounded in a revolutionary technology defined by speed and access, call for new skills among the prime practitioners of diplomacy:

- Because the power of communication is so broadly disseminated, the capacity to communicate effectively becomes ever more critical in pursuing diplomatic aims. The competition for mind space includes strong non-governmental players with cheap access to global audiences. The contest to sustain a credible position requires uncanny communication skills and individual stature

– one might suggest a capacity for durable celebrity (and so celebrities often pretend to diplomacy now).

- Because global communication is instantaneous and 24/7, the capacity to act and react quickly becomes a tactical requirement. The "back-office" for diplomacy must be small, closely tied to the leader, and capable of immediate response. (So-called war rooms in big electoral contests are an example of this.) Ironically, much wider dissemination of information and influence requires more centralization in the capacity to manage major files. The traditional diplomat is devalued in this context.

- Because digital technology dramatically undermines security of information, the advantage of "secret" data is significantly reduced, and may even be counter-productive. Indeed, credibility will rest to an unusual degree on transparency, if only because hypocrisy and duplicity are so much more likely to be revealed in the naked arena of action.

- Because the influence of unofficial actors in major events is so much greater than it was in the past, intelligence-gathering on nongovernmental players grows in relevance. This is required to help predict events, and to effectively engage third-party players in the multidimensional competition for advantage.

- Because the issues confronting diplomacy are now so often global in scope (environment, economy, health, terrorism), the knowledge base for leading players must be substantially enriched in various fields.

None of this means that we are receding to some "medieval chaos" characterized by no centres at all, but it does require skill sets for diplomacy that are unique to our time, and uniquely demanding.

In the digital age – building on the industrial age – we move from the some to the many, from the stately to the frenetic, from command to influence, from deception to candour, and from interests to issues. This suggests that diplomats cupboard the gin – or double their rations – and that we should try to tempt Allan Gotlieb back to the fold.

Contributors

Janice Gross Stein is the Belzberg Professor of Conflict Management in the Department of Political Science and director of the Munk School of Global Affairs at the University of Toronto. She is a Fellow of the Royal Society of Canada, and a member of the Orders of Canada and of Ontario. Her most recent publications include *The Cult of Efficiency* (2001), *Street Protests and Fantasy Parks* (2001), and *The Unexpected War: Canada in Kandahar* (2007) (co-author). She was the Massey Lecturer in 2001 and has been awarded the Molson Prize by the Canada Council for outstanding contributions by a social scientist to public debate. She is an honourary foreign member of the American Academy of Arts and Sciences. Janice lives in Toronto.

Robert Bothwell is the May Gluskin Professor of Canadian History at the University of Toronto, and director of the university's International Relations Program at Trinity College. A former editor of the *Canadian Historical Review*, he is the author of *The Penguin History of Canada* and numerous books on atomic energy, international affairs, and political history.

Sondra Gotlieb is a journalist and novelist. She is married to Allan Gotlieb, former Canadian ambassador to the United States. Her book *Washington Rollercoaster* recounted the Gotliebs' years as glamorous hosts in Washington during the Reagan era, when she wrote a much-read column, called

"Wife Of," for the *Washington Post*. She has published several books, both fiction and non-fiction, including the 1978 Leacock Medal–winning novel *True Confections*. Two of her other books have been finalists for the prize. Her most recent book, *When I Rises Up, I Gets Confused*, is a collection of essays spanning thirty years of her writing. She lives in Toronto.

Marc Lortie is Canada's ambassador to France. He joined the Department of External Affairs in 1971. He served abroad in Tunisia (1973–75) and Washington (1979–83), and was seconded to the Prime Minister's Office in 1985 where he was in charge of relations with the international media until 1987 when he was named press secretary. In 1989, he returned to the diplomatic service and served in Paris as Minister-Counsellor for Political Affairs and as Personal Representative of the Prime Minister for La Francophonie. He was named Canadian ambassador to Chile in 1993; in 1997 he was nominated Fellow at the Centre for International Affairs at Harvard University. He returned to Ottawa in September 1998 when he was appointed sherpa for the third summit of the Americas, and in 2001 he was appointed assistant deputy minister for the Americas. He was Canada's ambassador to Spain from 2004 to 2007.

Colin Robertson is a senior strategic advisor for McKenna, Long and Aldridge LLP. He is Vice President and Senior Research Fellow at the Canadian Defence and Foreign Affairs Institute. He is an honourary captain (Navy) assigned to the Strategic Communications Directorate. A career Foreign Service officer from 1977 to 2010, he served as first head of the advocacy secretary and minister at the Canadian embassy in Washington, as consul general in Los Angeles, with previous assignments in Hong Kong and in New York at the UN and Consulate General. He was a member of the team that negotiated the Canada-U.S. FTA and NAFTA.

Brian Bow is an associate professor of political science at Dalhousie University, and is currently (2010–11) a Senior Fellow at the Center for North American Studies at American University. He is the author of *The Politics of Linkage: Power, Interdependence and Ideas in Canada-US Relations*, which was awarded the Donner Prize as best public policy book published in Canada in 2009. He is also the co-editor of *An Independent Foreign Policy for Canada? Challenges and Choices for the Future* (2008), and various articles and chapters on Canada-U.S. relations, Canadian foreign policy, and North American regional politics. He has been a visiting researcher at the Woodrow Wilson Center, Georgetown University, Carleton University, and Australian National University.

From 1992 to 2006, **Jeremy Kinsman** was a Canadian ambassador or high commissioner in Moscow, Rome, London, and Brussels (EU), accredited to fifteen countries. Earlier, he was minister for political affairs at the Canadian embassy, Washington, and deputy permanent representative to the UN, New York. Today, he directs an international democracy support project for the Community of Democracies (www.diplomatshandbook.org). He is lead writer for foreign affairs for *Policy Options* magazine, and writes for cbc.ca/news and other outlets. Recently diplomat-in-residence at Princeton University, he holds current academic positions as resident international scholar at the Institute of Governmental Studies at the University of California, Berkeley, and as distinguished visiting diplomat at Ryerson University, Toronto.

David Malone is president of Canada's International Development Research Centre (IDRC). Previously Canada's high commissioner to India and earlier a Canadian ambassador at the UN, he has written extensively about peace and security issues. His most recent book is *Does the Elephant Dance?: Contemporary Indian Foreign Policy* (2011).

Elissa Golberg is currently the director general of the Stabilization and Reconstruction Task Force (START) in the Department of Foreign Affairs and International Trade, a position she has held since April 2009. She has also served as the representative of Canada in Kandahar, the executive director of the Independent Panel on Canada's Future Role in Afghanistan (the "Manley Panel"), senior director of START and director of the Humanitarian Affairs and Disaster Response Division. Ms. Golberg has participated in the management of Canadian government responses to several conflicts and natural disasters including most recently as the co-coordinator of the Government of Canada's 2010 Haiti earthquake task force. She is a recipient of the NATO ISAF General Service medal, the Queen's Jubilee Medal, the Public Service Award of Excellence, three Minister's Awards for Foreign Policy Excellence, and was named a Young Global Leader by the World Economic Forum in 2010. She has published several articles on humanitarian and stabilization matters.

Michael Kaduck is director, Europe Division, in the International Assessment Staff of the Privy Council Office. Prior to joining PCO in 2011, Mr. Kaduck was a Foreign Service officer for over seventeen years, serving abroad in Pakistan and the Caribbean, and in Ottawa including as director of the Peace Operations and Fragile States Policy Division in the Stabilization and Reconstruction Task Force (START) at DFAIT. A graduate of Queen's University at Kingston and the University of Calgary, Mr. Kaduck has published a number of articles in *bout de papier* magazine, and one in the edited collection *Canadian Political Life: An Alberta Perspective*. He resides in Ottawa with his family.

Kim Richard Nossal is the Sir Edward Peacock Professor of International Relations and director of the Centre for International and Defence Policy at Queen's University. He is the author of a number of works on Canadian foreign and defence policy; his latest book, co-authored with Stéphane Roussel and Stéphane Paquin, is *International Policy and Politics in Canada* (2011).

Drew Fagan was assistant deputy minister for strategic policy and planning at the Department of Foreign Affairs and International Trade from 2006 to 2009. He is now Deputy Minister of Infrastructure and Deputy Minister Responsible for Seniors with the Government of Ontario. The views expressed are his alone, and do not reflect those of the Canadian or Ontario Governments. He would like to thank Logan St. John Smith, of the inaugural graduate program at the Munk School of Global Affairs, for his very able research assistance.

Edward Greenspon is vice-president of Business Development at the *Toronto Star* and Star Media Group. He was editor-in-chief of the *Globe and Mail* and globeandmail.com from 2002 to 2009, responsible for all content produced on all platforms. He has a combined honours degree in journalism and political science from Carleton University and was a Commonwealth Scholar at the London School of Economics. He chaired the GPS Project, an initiative of the Canadian International Council, and wrote its highly acclaimed report, "Open Canada, A Global Positioning Strategy for a Networked Age." He is co-author of two books, *Double Vision: The Inside Story of the Liberals in Power,* and *Searching for Certainty: Inside the New Canadian Mindset.*

Denis Stairs, O.C., F.R.S.C., is Professor Emeritus in Political Science and a Faculty Fellow of the Centre for Foreign Policy Studies (CFPS) at Dalhousie University. A former president of the Canadian Political Science Association, he was the founding director of the CFPS, and served as Dalhousie's vice-president (Academic and Research) from 1988 to 1993. Appointed to the Canadian Forces College Board of Visitors at its inception in 2002, he served as its chair from 2005 until 2009. He is a Senior Fellow with the Canadian Defence and Foreign Affairs Institute and the chair of its advisory council. A member of the board of directors of the Pearson Peacekeeping Centre, he specializes in Canadian foreign and defence policy, Canada-U.S. relations, and similar subjects.

George Haynal is a private sector executive with extensive experience in state-to-state diplomacy as a career officer in the Canadian foreign service.

Andrew Cohen, a native of Montreal, attended the Choate School, McGill University, and the University of Cambridge. Among his bestselling books are *Trudeau's Shadow: The Life and Legacy of Pierre Elliott Trudeau, The Unfinished Canadian: The People We Are,* and *While Canada Slept: How We Lost Our Place in the World,* a finalist for the Governor General's Literary Award. A former foreign correspondent and award-winning editorialist with the *Globe and Mail,* he has worked in Toronto, Washington, and Berlin. He writes a nationally syndicated column for the *Ottawa Citizen* and appears often on television and radio. The founding president of the Historica-Dominion Institute, he is a professor of journalism and international affairs at Carleton University in Ottawa.

Arif Lalani is the director-general of policy staff for the Department of Foreign Affairs and International Trade Canada, and a Senior Visiting Fellow at the Munk School of Global Affairs, University of Toronto. He has a B.A. from the University of British Columbia, and an M.Sc. in Management, Organisations and Governance from the London School of Economics. He served as the Canadian ambassador to Afghanistan, Jordan, and Iraq; he has also been posted to Turkey (with accreditation to Georgia and Azerbaijan), and to New York (as Alternative Representative to the Security Council) and Washington, D.C. In Ottawa, he has worked in the office of the senior advisor for the Middle East Peace Process; as coordinator for the Balkans; and as director, South Asia. He was the founder and chairperson of the foreign ministry's Working Group on Relations with Muslim Communities from 2005 to 2006. His current interests focus on bringing private sector Open Innovation practices to the public sector.

He serves on the advisory boards of the Munk School of Global Affairs, University of Toronto; the LSE project on business model innovation; and the Canadian Ditchley Foundation.

After twenty-five years in newspaper journalism, where he served for more than ten years as editor-in-chief of the *Globe and Mail,* **William Thorsell** was appointed director and CEO of the Royal Ontario Museum in August, 2000. During his tenure at the *Globe,* the newspaper won significant awards for design, journalistic excellence, public service, and marketing. He also wrote book reviews for *Report on Business* magazine and continues to contribute occasionally to the *Globe.* At the ROM, he led the museum's Renaissance ROM project, which saw the construction or renovation of more than 350,000 square feet of galleries, education facilities, and public amenities by 2010, including the renovation of several heritage buildings and the construction of the Michael Lee-Chin Crystal, designed by Daniel Libeskind. He was invested into the Order of Ontario in 2008 and was made a Chevalier of the Order of Arts and Letters of France in 2010. He lives in Toronto and in the Township of Mulmur in Dufferin County, Ontario.